New Life in the Wasteland

Dedication

Since these lectures were delivered in Scotland, it seems appropriate to dedicate them to three Scottish ministers, whose lives and preaching from three decades ago still push my own ministry in a heavenward direction:

To: The Reverend James Philip,
Minister Emeritus,
Holyrood Abbey Church of Scotland, Edinburgh

To the memory of:

The Reverend William Still,
late Minister of Gilcomston South Church of Scotland, Aberdeen

and

The Reverend Donald Lamont,
late Minister of St Columba's Free Church of Scotland, Edinburgh

'*whose faith follow...*' Hebrews 13:7 (AV)

New Life in the Wasteland

2 Corinthians on the Cost and Glory of Christian Ministry

'So then, death is at work in us, but life is at work in you'

2 Corinthians 4:12

Douglas F Kelly

Rutherford House

CHRISTIAN FOCUS

ISBN 1-85792-903-9

Published in 2003
by
Christian Focus Publications
Geanies House, Fearn, Tain, Ross-shire
IV20 1TW, Great Britain
and
Rutherford House,
17 Claremont Park, Edinburgh,
EH6 7PJ, Great Britain

www.christianfocus.com
Cover Design by Alister MacInnes

Printed and bound by Cox & Wyman, Reading

CONTENTS

Foreword

One of the bonuses as Warden of Rutherford House over the past ten years has been the annual pleasure of accompanying our distinguished Rutherford House Week speakers in their travels from one Scottish city to the next. It has been a great blessing to have fellowship with them as, beginning early each morning, we have eaten up the miles on the road to the day's engagements. Added to that delight has been the far greater privilege of then sitting at each speaker's feet, listening to them ministering to ministers at the morning gatherings and expounding the Word of God to the friends of the House in the evenings.

Not least memorable of these hectic weeks of meetings was the year when our guest speaker was Professor Douglas Kelly of Reformed Theological Seminary, North Carolina. Douglas spared nothing of himself as he poured out his heart each morning to the goodly company of those who came looking for encouragement and sustenance in that highest of callings – preaching the unsearchable riches of Christ. It was as a pastor that he spoke to pastors.

This little book has brought back fond memories of his moving ministry. In his thirteen addresses Dr Kelly showed himself to be fully in touch with our current secular culture; clearly he was acutely aware of the immense challenge every preacher faces today. But he also revealed a heart on fire for the glory of God, and he preached as one with a passion to declare the living Word. I believe nothing of that fiery passion has been lost in the preparation of the manuscript for publication, drawn as it has been from the sound recordings made of each address.

The Second Letter to the Corinthians was well chosen for a series of addresses to those in full-time Christian ministry. My only disappointment at the time the addresses were delivered was that each gathering heard only one of the expositions. My prayer is that the geographical limitation of Douglas' ministry will be made good by this publication: now the entire week's labour in the gospel can be put into the hands of many more than those who came to benefit from the gifts God has entrusted to his servant.

Within this book, the reader will find a rare model of expository preaching. Faithful to the text, Douglas brings the meaning of the great themes of 2 Corinthians right into the twenty-first century. He demonstrates that Reformed theology is completely relevant to contemporary culture. His is the gift of lifting the great apostle's thoughts and experiences and transferring them into 'light' and 'salt' for the church today. This is a book for ministers about their congregations; it also a book for congregations about their ministers! Indeed, it will be a hard heart that is not deeply moved and renewed by the reading of *New Life in theWasteland*. Pastors will be inspired to pray for their people, and believers will be driven to pray for their pastors!

I want to express my profound thanks to Douglas for his ready co-operation in checking the revision of the manuscript. Also my thanks to Alison Carter who with patience and meticulous care undertook the groundwork of that revision. Those of my staff at Rutherford House who have been involved in preparing this volume for publication join with Douglas Kelly in praying that God will graciously use this book for his glory and for encouragement of his people.

David C Searle
Rutherford House, Edinburgh
August, 2003

1

Decaying Western Culture

The context of contemporary ministry

T S Eliot titled one of his works *The Waste Land*. Much of our Western culture seems to be just that: a barren desert, denuded of life by 'the acids of modernism', ill prepared to cope with the challenge of resurgent Islam, and now even more confused by the contradictory complexities of philosophical pluralism spawned by post-modernism. Into this moribund, desert-like culture, the Christian church is called to minister nothing less than resurrection life. Of our best efforts we may ask at times with Eliot:

> That corpse you planted last year in your garden,
> Has it begun to sprout? Will it bloom this year?

Always bearing in mind what makes the corpse sprout, it is important to stand back a while as we enter the third millennium after Christ, and contemplate just what is the position of the gospel ministry today, in view of our deeply diseased Western culture.

Contemporary culture

Granted the severe limitations of our fallen human minds – some of the darkness of the Fall is still present even in the redeemed understanding – one has to be careful, humble and provisional in attempting to state precisely where God's pilgrim church is on her journey home. We cannot always judge by the superficial appearance of the church, because historically and theologically it is so often true that God is doing the most when things look the very worst. As Christ says in John 12:24, 'Unless a corn of wheat falls to the ground and dies, it remains only a single seed. But if it dies, it produces many seeds.' Often when the church seems buried and things seem most discouraging, God is working profoundly beneath the surface; I do not doubt that is happening in our culture in more respects than we may know today. Nevertheless, bearing this limitation of the human viewpoint in mind, we need to consider the duties and the possibilities of Christian ministry in what so many people call the 'post-Christian culture'. God has providentially called us to be born in this culture; he calls us to serve him gladly in the only place we can serve God on earth, not to long for some earlier or later culture.

When the nineteenth century turned into the twentieth century, a new religious periodical, which still continues, was started in New York City. It was optimistically entitled *The Christian Century*, emblematic of the whole thinking of the Protestant churches of that time. In a glorious sense that has been true in many areas outside the Western world – in parts of Korea and Africa, for instance. We thank God that for many of those places, it has indeed been the Christian century. Yet in our historically Christianised Europe and America, I do not think many could doubt that the twentieth century has been the opposite of the Christian century for our cultures. To an appalling degree, Europe, Britain and the United States have become secularised and paganised, prosperous though we have become. I suggest that the root of the problem of the secularisation of the West is a theological and spiritual one – that we have turned from the living, triune God to the service of idols.

An ineffective church

The last forty years have seen the British culture moving away from the gospel held by our forefathers; in the United States we have experienced exactly the same cultural shift as has been seen in Britain. From the 1960s to the 90s we have seen a massive secularisation of American life. Oddly enough, church attendance is still as high in most of the United States as it was in the 1920s and 30s. Recent statistics from a secular polling organisation indicated that about 42 percent of our population still frequent some kind of a church on any given Sunday. The strange fact is that American church attendance, impressive though it is, seems to have had very little influence on the actual culture. It has been unable to reverse the slide into secularism and paganism that is inundating the American culture, just as it is in Britain where church attendance is less than 10 percent. Thus we have to question the effectiveness of gospel ministry and church life on both sides of the Atlantic.

A disintegrating culture

I do not believe it would be very hard to convince most observers, whether they were conservative, liberal or moderate, that our society in the West is profoundly diseased. For a correct diagnosis, one must first be able to know the signs of good health, both physical and mental. Then you can more accurately spot what is wrong. It is the same with counterfeit money; banks train people to spot counterfeits by having them observe closely and repeatedly true pound notes, euros or dollar bills. Similarly, in order to diagnose what is wrong, we must first ask the question, 'What is the proper wholesome relationship of human beings with Almighty God?'

If we wish to summarise the entirety of the written Word of God, surely we could say that both the Old and New Testaments are covenants. The two parts of this book are bound together by the concept of God's one covenant of grace with sinful humanity in sovereign mercy: he plans that we should be his, allows the Fall, puts human beings as part of the plan, intervenes as the trinitarian God in his redemptive mercy, and ultimately sends down the new Jerusalem where he will be our God and we will be his people. By his inexplicable grace he chooses to be our God and he chooses us to be his people.

The essence of the covenant of grace is that we know God, as we see in Jeremiah 31:31-34, taken up in Hebrews 8:6-11; he is our God and we are his people and as such we know him. When the culture is rotting and breaking down, it is because the people do not know God. The word 'know' must be given its full biblical sense of personal relationship, intimate trust, deepest fidelity, tenderest communion. The Authorised Version of Genesis 4:1 tells us that Adam 'knew' his wife and they had offspring. The Lord Jesus says in John 17:3, 'Now this is eternal life: that they may know you, the only true God, and Jesus Christ, whom you have sent.' Salvation and health are ultimately *knowing* God. The sanctity of the human marital relationship is a reflection of this most precious and crucial form of 'knowing'.

A definition of idolatry

Essentially this is the disaster of our culture, that instead of knowing God, our people know idols. We are called to minister in a time that is characterised by idolatry more than anything else, and this was the problem at Corinth too. What is idolatry? It is a vicious, heartless rejection of the noble, generous and tender Lover to whose infinite mercy and affection the otherwise helpless beloved owes absolutely everything. That is how God sees idolatry. That is why he reacts against it so powerfully and sent a whole people into captivity for it.

It is described very vividly in Ezekiel 16. There God found an abandoned baby of pagan parents, fresh from her own unwanted birth, still wallowing in blood in the open field, where she had been left to die alone. Of course, in our day where we are more progressive, this baby girl would have already had her life terminated in an abortion clinic and been burned in the incinerator. But in more primitive times, she was just abandoned. God takes her up and washes her, nourishes her, clothes her, bringing her up with royal care until at length she becomes a beautiful young woman whom he takes as his wife. This, of course, is a foreshadowing of Christ's love for his church in Ephesians 5:23-32.

However, this beautiful but thankless young woman trusted in her own beauty (not unlike Lucifer himself, who at the dawn of time seems to have fallen because he was enraptured with his own splendid appearance). Rather than gazing on the face of her true, noble Lover, she focuses on herself so that her love is transmuted into lust; Ezekiel 16:15 says: 'You lavished your favours on anyone who passed by and your beauty became his.' Her illicit sexual pleasures were, as they still are today in every sinful relationship, subject to the law of diminishing returns. As with drugs, you have to do more to get the required effect. The further her whoredoms went, the more degenerate she became. She ultimately stooped to the low point of hiring enemy nations and paying them to sleep with her (Ezek. 16:33). God's judgement upon his whoring wife would be national disaster: 'Then I will hand you over to your lovers, and they will tear down your mounds and destroy your lofty shrines. They will strip you of your clothes and take your fine jewellery and leave you naked and bare. They will bring a mob against you, who will stone you and hack you to pieces with their swords. They will burn down your houses and inflict punishment on you in the sight of many women. I will put a stop to your prostitution, and you will no longer pay your lovers' (Ezek. 16:39-41).

A hundred years before Ezekiel and Jeremiah, the book of Hosea describes the national degeneracy of the idolatrous northern kingdom of Israel, illustrated by the personal unfaithfulness of

Hosea's adulterous wife, Gomer. She went from bad to worse, plunging to such depths of lust and depravity that finally she had to be sold into the debauched slavery of actual prostitution. Eventually, in the amazing love of God, her husband goes and buys this totally unworthy person back. This incident gives us hope for any culture, I believe.

An idol-ridden culture

A crucial principle about the nature of idol worship is that persistent spiritual idolatry leads to intellectual and physical adultery, then on to other kinds of mental and sexual perversion. It is important to note here that there are more kinds of idolatry than literally bowing to images of Baal, or taking part in orgiastic rituals in the groves of Ashtoreth. If we do not realise this, I think we will not be able to analyse properly the ravaging cancer of our times and the culture in which we have to minister, raise our own children and live our own lives. Because we may not see actual idol statues, we must never imagine that our culture is idol-free.

Let me illustrate what I mean about the multi-faceted nature of modern idolatry. Professor Herbert Schlossberg has written a perceptive book entitled *Idols for Destruction – the Conflict of Christian Faith and American Culture*. He classifies an idol as any value or principle that men substitute for God. He shows that there are two general kinds of idols – idols of nature and idols of history. He shows that these idols of whatever description inevitably lead to the destruction of those who follow them, echoing the words of Hosea 8:4, 'They make idols for themselves to their own destruction.' God must judge that culture which turns its back on him and bases its life on false gods, defined as some other kind of value that is put in his place.

The Bible, history and contemporary life all illustrate that spiritual idolatry and intellectual treason inevitably lead to widespread sexual degeneracy. What is the reason for the amazing sexual emphasis of our culture? The relationship between idolatry and adultery is complicated, but the basic connection is clear. Intellectual rejection of God and sexual immorality are very closely intertwined; one may say of them what John Calvin says in Book 1 of his *Institutes of the Christian Religion* about the human personality's knowledge of self and its knowledge of God. Calvin says that our knowledge of self and our knowledge of God are so profoundly intertwined that psychologically it is impossible to tell where one begins and the other ends and which one comes first. Perhaps the same is true in regard to the matter of idolatry and adultery.

The question is this: do people commit wholesale adultery because they have grown cold on God, like a marriage going sour? A husband or wife does not usually seek out another partner if the marriage is successful and warm; they go outside if it has gone cold. So, do people commit wholesale adultery because they have first grown cold towards God or do they reject God (as we see the intellectual and cultural leadership of our countries trying to hold back the evidences of God's reality in what they report in the media) precisely in order to commit adultery and other forms of sexual licence? Which is first? Thomas Aquinas may have been pointing in the right direction when he said in the thirteenth century: 'Unchastity's first-born daughter is blindness of spirit.'

Robbing the Creator of his glory

In the inspired analysis of the apostle Paul in Romans 1:18, 'The wrath of God is being revealed from heaven against all the godlessness and wickedness of men who suppress [literally "hold down"] the truth by their wickedness.' In other words, it is not that our culture does not know there is a God, and does not have some kind of a moral monitor in their conscience. They do, and they know far more than they are willing to let on, which is one of the encouragements in preaching the gospel. When you preach the Word of God, even to a liberal, cynical, sarcastic person, there is something in them that they are not entirely able to cancel out. Paul builds a case that the reality of God's existence and holy demands on all people may be clearly perceived from creation about us and conscience within us. But because of our sinful hearts, instead of truly knowing and glorifying God (Rom. 1:21) we pervert our Creator's glory and replace him with corruptible idols from the idol factory of the human mind. God then gives such an idolatrous culture up to 'the sinful desires of their hearts' (v. 24). The appalling personal and societal consequences of this blindness of spirit which is the first-born daughter of unchastity, are catalogued in Romans 1:26-28.

One of the most brilliant analyses of the empowering of the sexual licentiousness of modern Western culture by its theological apostasy and intellectual idolatry, was given years ago by Jean Brun who is now Professor Emeritus at the University of Dijon, in a book entitled in French *Le Retour de Dionysius (The Return of Dionysius)*. The same theme was taken up in a book of much insight, published in 1993, entitled *Degenerate Moderns – Modernity As Rationalised Sexual Misbehaviour* by an American Roman Catholic, E Michael Jones. Although the last chapter, in my view, totally misrepresents the life and teaching of Luther, I believe this book gives us a great deal of insight into why our culture is where it is, and can even help us know how Christian ministry, with the grace of God, can reverse it.

Conforming truth to desire

This is what Jones says: 'There are ultimately only two alternatives in the intellectual life. Either one conforms desire to the truth, or one conforms truth to desire.' That is, truly to know God entails mortification of lust. As we mortify lust by God's grace with the help of the Holy Spirit, then that is succeeded by daily resurrections to something higher and better in one's personal existence. But on the other hand, those who refuse to conform their desires to the truth, are like Ephraim in Hosea 4:17-18: 'Ephraim is joined to idols; leave him alone! Even when their drinks are gone, they continue their prostitution; their rulers dearly love shameful ways.' They lower God and then deny God, all the better to replace him with new gods who will not rebuke them for morally collapsing before the onslaught of their own lusts.

Paul Johnson has written an interesting biography of the largely immoral leaders of our modern intelligentsia entitled *The Intellectuals*. These three authors – Brun, Jones and Johnson – demonstrate that the latter course, the conforming of the truth to human natural lust, has been the story of Western civilisation since the eighteenth-century French Enlightenment, which was based so heavily on seventeenth-century English deism. This shows the uncomfortable and disturbing fact that ours is an idolatrous culture because it is an adulterous culture. Well might Hosea 4:17 be written on the lintels over the mighty doors of universities, broadcasting networks, publishing houses, stock exchanges and halls of civil government: 'Ephraim is joined to idols; leave him alone!'

Rationalised misbehaviour

Jones states it bluntly: the thesis of this book is simple – modernity was rationalised sexual misbehaviour. All the intellectual and cultural breakthroughs of modernity were, in some way or other, linked to the sexual desires their progenitors knew to be illicit but which they chose nonetheless. Their theories were ultimately rationalisations of the choices they knew to be wrong. Jones goes into details from Margaret Meade, talks about some of the things in the life of the liberal theologian Paul Tillich, and describes the morals of the Bloomsbury group, Freud, Kinsey and others. He regards as plausible the claim that there is only one generator of urban modernity in the West – sexual licence, of which homosexual practice is merely a subset.

The sexual immorality of Cairns, Strachey, Forster and the Bloomsbury group of the 1920s in Cambridge was presumably restricted to a relatively small elite in Western culture. But what was hidden in the 1920s has come out of the closet and is now stalking the streets of our cities, our schools, media and art. The ethics of the closet could not have moved to the moderatorial chair on centre stage, as it were, had not our idolatrous-adulterous culture constantly adjusted its views of truth to conform to its unmortified lusts over the last seventy or eighty years. If Brun, Johnson, Schlossberg and Jones are right, it is because of unbridled lust that our late twentieth-century culture is so deeply sunk into the depravity that always follows the blindness of spirit, which increases the longer idolatry is practised.

These lines written by Alexander Pope in his *Essay on Man* say a great deal:

> Vice is a monster of so frightful mien,
> As, to be hated, needs but to be seen;
> Yet seen too oft, familiar with her face,
> We first endure, then pity, then embrace.

Decades ago, Carl Mannheim, a German sociologist, stated, 'Civilisation is collapsing before our eyes.' 'If God is dead,' said Dostoyevsky, 'everything is permitted.' I believe that a large part of God's judgement on our idolatrous culture is to let it take the logical consequences of the horrendous choices it has made in abandoning him, the framework of his saving gospel, and his holy, secure law.

Sections of the church have played a large part in this drift away from God. C E M Joad saw that the Church of England was being transformed by the process of accommodating the views of naturalism and materialism. He accused it of becoming a mere purveyor of vague, ethical, religious uplift. Once G K Chesterton said of America, 'It is a nation with the soul of a church.' 'Yes,' replied Alistair Cooke, 'it's true, but it also has the soul of a whorehouse.' The Old Testament reminds us that when prophet and priest are corrupted, cultural disaster cannot be far behind. Amos says there is no famine like a 'famine of hearing the words of the Lord' (Amos 8:11). Yet no matter how bad our cultural collapse, God can change it; his gospel is competent to handle it, as we shall see in our study of Paul's Second Letter to the Church in Corinth.

2

The Value of Pain and Suffering

2: 2 Cor 1:1-11

[1]Paul, an apostle of Christ Jesus by the will of God, and Timothy our brother, To the church of God in Corinth, together with all the saints throughout Achaia: [2]Grace and peace to you from God our Father and the Lord Jesus Christ.

[3]Praise be to the God and Father of our Lord Jesus Christ, the Father of compassion and the God of all comfort, [4]who comforts us in all our troubles, so that we can comfort those in any trouble with the comfort we ourselves have received from God. [5]For just as the sufferings of Christ flow over into our lives, so also through Christ our comfort overflows. [6]If we are distressed, it is for your comfort and salvation; if we are comforted, it is for your comfort, which produces in you patient endurance of the same sufferings we suffer. [7]And our hope for you is firm, because we know that just as you share in our sufferings, so also you share in our comfort.

[8]We do not want you to be uninformed, brothers, about the hardships we suffered in the province of Asia. We were under great pressure, far beyond our ability to endure, so that we despaired even of life. [9]Indeed, in our hearts we felt the sentence of death. But this

happened that we might not rely on ourselves but on God, who raises the dead. [10]He has delivered us from such a deadly peril, and he will deliver us. On him we have set our hope that he will continue to deliver us, [11]as you help us by your prayers. Then many will give thanks on our behalf for the gracious favor granted us in answer to the prayers of many.

The apostle Paul's ministry took place against the background of a rotting Hellenistic culture; when you read what the classical writers really said, it is amazing how corrupt and degenerate their culture was. Undoubtedly the achievements of the Graeco-Roman world were very great, but the way they treated one another was appalling. This is the setting in which Paul sees all the idols in Athens in Acts 17:16. In Acts 18 Paul is in Corinth, where he has to deal with the issues that arise when people get converted yet are still profoundly influenced by the pagan immorality that pervades an idolatrous culture. Corinth was a place where the worship of Aphrodite was practised and there was widespread cult prostitution. When the classical playwrights of the ancient world wanted to represent a man as a drunkard or a lecher, they would say that he came from Corinth.

Into that situation came Paul, a man who knew not idols, but the living God, and was sold out to him. Paul preached first in the Jewish synagogue in Corinth, as was his custom. Some folk were saved and the controversy started; Paul was kicked out of the synagogue, then went to Titius Justus' house. Later, when many people were being converted, there was a huge riot. The whole city in some way was involved, and he was called before Gallio, the pro-consul who was the brother of Seneca. He survived that encounter; God was working even when it looked as if the idolaters were going to kill him. Because the resurrection is more powerful than death, God was working. That is why we must never be discouraged no matter how bad it looks outwardly. When we are bringing God's Word, when we are sold out to Jesus Christ, God is working.

So that was the beginning of Paul's time in Corinth. It was a church that seems to have given him far more pain than even the Galatian church, yet the grace that is shown in 1 and 2 Corinthians is most remarkable. Paul wrote four letters to Corinth, of which two were lost and two have been preserved. In a previous letter Paul had upset some of the church by telling them not to associate with immoral persons; it encouraged me as a minister to know that even a mighty apostle had made people in his congregation angry with him!

After this letter was misunderstood, he wrote the letter that we know as 1 Corinthians to deal with disorders and to answer questions brought by Chloe's household. This second letter did seem to do some good in that emotionally charged situation, but still he was getting some rather negative reports in Corinth. Then, out of much affliction and anguish, he sent a third sorrowful letter which seems to have been lost. But afterwards the apostle received good news from Titus that things were a little better. Paul made a visit to Corinth but the situation was so bad that he had to hot-foot it out of town, yet he received some reports that his visit had helped. Then he wrote a letter to express relief that the situation had improved; this was the fourth letter he wrote to the Corinthians, the one we know as 2 Corinthians. Paul was glad that his dealings with the church at Corinth had made things somewhat better. But he still had to deal with the problems of ministering in an idolatrous, adulterous culture.

There were people there who wanted to turn the congregation against Paul, because they wanted to be in charge. They were spreading lies against God's servant, saying 'he promised he would visit us, but he did not; he is fickle so we cannot depend on his message.' So his whole ministry was on the line; he had to defend his ministry in order to defend the very gospel that he preached. Also he wanted the church at Corinth, which was apparently well-endowed financially, to give an offering to the needy saints in Jerusalem.

I would suggest that 2 Corinthians divides into three major parts: the first part in chapters 1–7 deals with the apostle's ministry; the second part in chapters 8, 9 and part of 10 discusses plans for an offering; the third part in chapters 10–13 is a vindication of Paul's apostleship. In chapter 1:1-11 Paul writes about the value of difficulties, pain and suffering that God may call us to endure from time to time in our Christian service. The Lord mingles our cup very tenderly and graciously with joy and sorrow, testing and pleasure. But from time to time he does call every true servant of his to go through dark places; it is especially this situation that seems to be in view in 2 Corinthians. The believers experienced the pressure that will come upon those who profess the truth, when it is unwelcome to those who want to conform the truth to their desires 'rather than conform their desires to the truth', to quote E Michael Jones.

The first main paragraph of chapter 1 (after the customary introductory greetings) is unusual. Normally the apostle dwells on God's blessing to the church, as he does in 1 Corinthians and 1 Thessalonians; here he does not dwell on what God has done in the lives of the Corinthians, but on what God had done in his own life. Now why does he take this tack in the introduction? The reason is that in verses 3-7 Paul is giving thanks for what God has done in his life in precise connection with the pain that these Corinthians had caused him. He is saying, 'You've hurt me but I can even thank God for the hurt that you caused me because good has come out of it.' It is a word of grace and forgiveness to this church; it takes a generous and big-hearted man to utter such a word. 'You hurt me but God has enlarged me through this and further blessings will come to the church through this.' Alexander Whyte has a wonderful essay on the apostle Paul as a gentleman.

Grace born out of difficulties

Sometimes we see an example of this graciousness when maybe a child apologises to a parent for having been so awful for some of their teen years. Yet the parent can say, 'Yes, but God was driving us to himself and teaching us more about himself and we can see that blessing came out of that.' Or maybe a parent who was abusive and mean comes to an adult child in later years to apologise, and the child can say, 'Yes, that was hurtful, and yet God drove me to himself and so grace has come out of it.'

When people cause us hurts and difficulties, we need to have this attitude of looking to God and asking, 'Now what is God doing in this?' Not so much, 'Why did he let it happen?' – 'Why?' is not the right question – but 'What is he saying, what is he doing, how could this further his grace in my life and that of others?' When we can ask that question, bitterness and divisiveness in the congregation cannot co-exist with such an attitude. In some ways the anti-authoritarianism of our times is healthy, but even legitimate authority is being undermined. Ministers suffer because of the resulting cynicism towards the clergy, but when we can look to God and ask him the question 'How can your grace be ministered even to those who are causing me difficulty?' then wonderful things can happen.

Paul mentions four values of difficulty and suffering in the service of Christ amongst the idolatrous-adulterous culture of Corinth, which we can apply to our own service amongst the countries of the largely apostate West.

Comfort in troubles

First, we learn *the value of suffering for the Lord*, when a man or woman of God is faithfully serving him. (We must be careful not to bring suffering upon ourselves through our own fault: for example, through foolishness, tactlessness or laziness.) Such faithful suffering connects believers in an especially close way with the thorn-crowned yet glory-crowned Redeemer. When we, in identity with the purposes of the Master, have to go through some hurt, it is then that God comforts us in all our tribulation, says Paul in verse 4. If we can say 'Let this cup pass from me; nevertheless, if this is the only way my people can be saved and your honour and integrity maintained, I will go through it', then we get very close to the Lord Jesus in some way that cannot be attained in the sunshine, much as we all love the sun. When we get to such a place we will not compromise because of our very closeness to the purposes of the Master, so our difficulties take on a redemptive value.

Let us be clear that we do not pay for our sins. The blood of Jesus Christ on the cross is the propitiation for our sins – not for ours only but for the whole world. The sins of all God's people of all ages are paid for in the blood of Christ. Yet in another sense a costly stand which hurts you and your family (such as maintaining the truth in a relativistic culture fiercely intolerant of truth-claims) can have a redemptive value because the cross you are experiencing becomes a doorway to let through the Lord's resurrection power into other lives. Paul seems to be speaking of this when he says in Colossians 1:24, 'I fill up in my flesh what is still lacking in regard to Christ's afflictions, for the sake of his body, which is the church.' Sometimes when you are feeling the nails, that may be the only way that others can see his glory.

Learning experientially

Secondly, *suffering for the Lord in his service brings a new revelation of who God really is*. I have said that the thing that characterises health is knowing God through the Bible – Genesis to Revelation. If this Bible is true, the most important question in the world is who God really is (v. 3). Now there are certain things about God which you can only learn experientially in the fire, and this reality goes with you when you come out of the fire. There is a saying in French that, when you translate it into English, goes something like this: 'To suffer, passes. To have suffered, never passes.' What you learn about the Lord in the fire goes with you blessedly long after you have left the fire. Some tests he may not call you through again in this whole earthly pilgrimage, but the effects go with you.

Paul also expressly tells us in verse 3 one of the things we learn most about God when we are under pressure for him: he is 'the Father of compassion and the God of all comfort'. Yes, his purity and his power are attributes of stupendous importance, but in the fire we find the comfort – a wonderful word meaning 'strong together'. It is perhaps a reflection of the light within the Holy Trinity. The comfort and the mercy of God come through in the fire; they do amazing things in us in a way that nothing else can. There is a tract about Christian service called *Tenderness of Spirit* which says that God has to let you mature and put you through some difficulties before he can use you more widely. One of the memorable sentences is: 'Out of the presses of pain cometh the soul's best wine.'

This is what Isabel Allison, one of the Covenanting Scottish women who would pay with her life, wrote on the 26th January 1681, after singing the 23rd Psalm and then the 84th Psalm, before she was taken to the scaffold: 'What shall I say to the commendation of Christ and His cross? I bless the Lord that He has made my prison a palace to me. And what am I that He should have dealt thus with me? I have looked greedy-like to such a lot as this but still thought it was too high for me, when I saw how vile I was.'

Samuel Rutherford when he was on his way to be jailed in Aberdeen, wrote a letter signed, 'In haste, making for my palace in Aberdeen.' By palace, he meant prison, but if the Lord Jesus was in it, it was a palace. How different from our materialistic way of thinking! He says in this letter: 'No king is better provided for than I am. Sweet, sweet and easy is the cross of my Lord. My chains are over-gilded with gold. No pen, no words, no genius can express to you the loveliness of my only Lord Jesus.' This experience of knowing comfort and mercy is through our Lord Jesus Christ whom we meet in the fire.

Comfort for others

Thirdly, in verses 4-6 we learn that *Christ's death as it works in us gives us new power to comfort others.* We do not go out and seek these 'deaths', but he lets the circumstances come upon us if we are seeking to minister for him. It is those who have been through a particular experience that often can help others the most; something is done in us to give us an authority from God to put strength and light in other people. In 2 Corinthians 4:10 Paul describes believers thus: 'We always carry around in our body the death of Jesus, so that the life of Jesus may also be revealed in our body.'

The great preacher, Charles Haddon Spurgeon, experienced many physical difficulties. His son, Charles Spurgeon Junior, wrote of him, 'I know of no one who could comfort more sweetly than my dear father, impart comfort to bleeding hearts and sad spirits. As the crushing of the flower causes it to yield its aroma, so he, having endured in a long continued illness of my beloved mother and also constant pains in himself, was able to sympathise most tenderly with all sufferers.'

Spurgeon tells a most amazing story in volume 2 of his autobiography *The Full Harvest*. In the course of speaking at a Monday evening prayer meeting at the Tabernacle, on the personal preparation of the soul in order to be used, Spurgeon said:

> Some years ago, I was the subject of fearful depression of spirit. I was also unwell and my heart sank within me. Out of the depths, I was forced to cry unto the Lord. Just before I went away to Menton for rest, I suffered greatly in body, but far more in soul, for my spirit was overwhelmed. Under this pressure I preached a sermon from the words, 'My God, my God why hast thou forsaken me?' I was as much qualified to preach from that text as ever I expected to be. Indeed, I hope that few of my brethren could have entered so deeply into those heartbreaking words. I felt to the full of my measure the horror of a soul forsaken of God. Now that was not a desirable experience. I tremble at the very idea of passing again through that eclipse of soul. But that night after the service, there

came into my vestry a man who was as nearly as insane as he could be outside of an asylum. His eyes seemed ready to start from his head and he said that he should have utterly despaired if he had not heard that discourse which had made him feel that there was one man alive who understood his feelings and could describe his experience.

Five years later Spurgeon said:

Now hear the sequel. Last night when of all the times of the year, strange to say, I was preaching from the words, 'The Almighty hath vexed my soul.' After the service, in walked this self-same brother who had called on me five years before. This time, he looked as different as noon-day from midnight or as alive from dead. I said to him, 'I am glad to see you for I have often thought about you and wondered whether you were brought into perfect peace.' To my inquiries this brother replied, 'Yes, you said five years ago that I was a hopeful patient and I am sure you will be glad to know that I have walked in the sunlight from that day till now. Everything has changed and altered with me.' Dear friends, as soon as I saw my poor despairing patient the first time, I blessed God that my fearful experiences had prepared me to sympathise with him, but last night when I saw him perfectly restored, my heart overflowed with gratitude. I would go into the deeps a hundred times to cheer a downcast spirit. It is good for me that I have been afflicted that I might know how to speak a word in season to one that is weary.

Room to trust in God

Fourthly, in verses 8-9, *suffering with and for Christ has a way of killing our self-centred thinking and leaving room for us to trust God who raises the dead.* It is interesting that one of the American television evangelists who got out of jail a few years ago has been quoted in the media as saying that the prosperity theology that he was previously teaching was a lie, and that he had been conforming the Bible to his desires. But God had done great things for him in the prison and now he wanted to conform himself to the Word of God.

We often ask, 'Why has something in our life, or indeed our life itself, fallen flat?' Sometimes God has to let every door slam in our ministerial face or our financial face or our physical face or whatever. Otherwise we might have relied on our intelligence, our beauty, our family, our cash, our whatever. So God closes every door and we are at the end of our resources. Then suddenly we realise that there is just one door; if anything is to happen it looks as if God will have to do it. Then God says, 'Well, child, isn't that the point? Haven't you been telling others that? Don't you think it will work for you?' That is when death works in us.

Even an apostle had to be brought to this place. Paul the mighty apostle had been up into the heavenly places and seen things he could not even reveal (12:2-4). There was no question in his mind – there is a heaven, there is a God and it is all true; he had seen it physically. But a man like that had to be brought to this place again and again. He had to be thrown back on God, to know that only the Lord could do it, and he had to die to himself so that the resurrection life of Jesus could get through.

This may be one reason the Lord has, in his providence, let the West go so secular in our lifetime and our parents' lifetime. Why are the media, the universities and governments generally so anti-Christian or, at least, tending in that direction? Could it be that it is to make us realise that we cannot do it, but that God will have to do it. Are we prepared to offer ourselves up that his resurrection glory might shine? When the heat comes on and when the pressure is such that we cannot handle it, we do not generally feel religious or see that the Lord Jesus is working. It might even seem as if God is doing so much for our enemies. But it is just at those times when we do not feel it or see it, that God is doing tremendous things. A power is stealing through that is far greater than all the forces of death and destruction, and that is able to revive the situation in this culture as it has in other past cultures: namely the resurrection power of the Lord Jesus Christ.

3

God's 'Yes' Conquers Humanity's 'No'

Cor 1:12-2:11

[12]Now this is our boast: Our conscience testifies that we have conducted ourselves in the world, and especially in our relations with you, in the holiness and sincerity that are from God. We have done so not according to worldly wisdom but according to God's grace. [13]For we do not write you anything you cannot read or understand. And I hope that, [14]as you have understood us in part, you will come to understand fully that you can boast of us just as we will boast of you in the day of the Lord Jesus.

[15]Because I was confident of this, I planned to visit you first so that you might benefit twice. [16]I planned to visit you on my way to Macedonia and to come back to you from Macedonia, and then to have you send me on my way to Judea. [17]When I planned this, did I do it lightly? Or do I make my plans in a worldly manner so that in the same breath I say, "Yes, yes" and "No, no"?

[18]But as surely as God is faithful, our message to you is not "Yes" and "No."[19]For the Son of God, Jesus Christ, who was preached among

you by me and Silas and Timothy, was not "Yes" and "No," but in him it has always been "Yes."[20] For no matter how many promises God has made, they are "Yes" in Christ. And so through him the "Amen" is spoken by us to the glory of God. [21] Now it is God who makes both us and you stand firm in Christ. He anointed us, [22] set his seal of ownership on us, and put his Spirit in our hearts as a deposit, guaranteeing what is to come.

[23] I call God as my witness that it was in order to spare you that I did not return to Corinth. [24] Not that we lord it over your faith, but we work with you for your joy, because it is by faith you stand firm.

[1] So I made up my mind that I would not make another painful visit to you. [2] For if I grieve you, who is left to make me glad but you whom I have grieved? [3] I wrote as I did so that when I came I should not be distressed by those who ought to make me rejoice. I had confidence in all of you, that you would all share my joy. [4] For I wrote you out of great distress and anguish of heart and with many tears, not to grieve you but to let you know the depth of my love for you.

[5] If anyone has caused grief, he has not so much grieved me as he has grieved all of you, to some extent—not to put it too severely. [6] The punishment inflicted on him by the majority is sufficient for him. [7] Now instead, you ought to forgive and comfort him, so that he will not be overwhelmed by excessive sorrow. [8] I urge you, therefore, to reaffirm your love for him. [9] The reason I wrote you was to see if you would stand the test and be obedient in everything. [10] If you forgive anyone, I also forgive him. And what I have forgiven—if there was anything to forgive—I have forgiven in the sight of Christ for your sake, [11] in order that Satan might not outwit us. For we are not unaware of his schemes.

In recent years I have often been in foreign countries where I have attended worship services conducted in languages of which I scarcely understood one word. Yet there is one word I always understand, whether pronounced in a Ukrainian, Romanian, Korean or Brazilian church. That is the universal word found in all Christian (and Jewish) worship: the word 'Amen'. The centre of this passage rests in the word 'Amen' which is derived from a Hebrew verb meaning 'so let it be', or 'so shall it be established'. When Abraham believed the Lord, he 'Amen-ed' the Lord in Genesis chapters 12, 15, 17 and 21. If we go back to Calvin, Aquinas, Anselm, Augustine and back to the Lord himself, back to the temple and back to Abraham – how many times have the people of God said the word 'Amen' as they have come to meet the living God? Every time we use the word 'Amen' we are entering into a heritage that is of the greatest importance. Our rootless culture needs to reconnect with this heritage.

The 'Amen' is a covenant word that speaks to us of the stability and security that the people of God have in the covenant of grace that runs all the way through the Scripture. It binds Old and New Testament together, given with increasing light and more glorious detail as we go through the patriarchs and through the prophets and on into the fullness of the revelation of the New Testament. When we say this word 'Amen', we are speaking of how secure is our standing in this wonderful covenant in which God has elected us. The word 'Amen' gathers up the whole covenant from beginning to end and says, 'You are secure in your Lord. Praise him for it. He will do it.' It is the opposite of the destruction that results from turning away from the true God to idolatry. By contrast, the 'Amen' speaks of upbuilding, of stability, of a future.

An unfulfilled promise

The first thing we note in this passage is that *Paul is speaking of 'Amen' in the context of promises*. He had made a promise to visit the Corinthian Christians which he had not been able to fulfil. Some of the people at Corinth who were resentful of Paul and his message used this as an excuse to attack his character and to undercut what he was trying to preach. They said that the apostle Paul was unstable, constantly changing his plans and not keeping his promises; all of this because in an earlier letter he had said he would visit Corinth soon. But Paul did not go immediately to Corinth and he tells us in verse 23 of chapter 1 the reason why he did not fulfil his promise. He refrained from going in order to spare them because he had already made a painful visit and he felt they were not ready yet for another whipping.

A wise minister will discern the times and judge when to rebuke and when to refrain. He will exercise tact in his dealings with his flock, so as not to exacerbate any problems, lest the church and the ministry be harmed. One of the sideeffects of people not submitting to God is that they will not submit to legitimate human authorities; thus they make it difficult for those placed with responsibility over them and they make it difficult for themselves. Wherever there is a faithful ministry in today's culture, it is very likely that those who begin feeling the authority of God coming through the preaching of the Word, will first of all start attacking the minister. Very seldom will they admit what the problem is and say, 'I don't agree with his preaching and I don't agree with the gospel and I don't like the God he's presenting.' They will start off by picking out something fairly minor – some flaw or something they do not like in him – and magnify it as a way to get away from the pressure to submit to the message. But if he persists and stays in there and they cannot work it that way, eventually they will probably come out and say they do not like the message. But that is nothing new. The apostle Paul encountered this and it is instructive to see how he dealt with it.

God's promises

Secondly, we note that Paul shows that *God fulfils all of his promises to us in Jesus Christ*, even though Paul was not able to fulfil a promise he had sincerely made. He says, 'I'm going to give you a contrast. I was not able to fulfil my promise to you and it's good I didn't, although you shouldn't use it to undercut my character and my message as some are doing' (vv. 15-18). Then he says, 'But let's look at God. God always fulfils the promises of his written word to us, his people' (v. 18f.). Then characteristically Paul engages in a bit of irony and says, 'The very reason I had to change my plans is because God never changes his plans. I had to cut out this visit to Corinth because of God's unchanging plan for his people in Corinth to bless them and to use me to bring a blessing. If I had come with the situation the way it was before you had done some changing, I would have brought a rod of punishment. So I changed my plans because God had something better for you' (v. 23f.). 'Some of you,' Paul says, 'are accusing me of speaking out of both sides of my mouth', to use a popular expression. 'But God only speaks one word. God only speaks out of one side of his mouth to his people. You accuse me of saying "yes" sometimes and "no" sometimes, but I want you to look at the God who always says "yes" to all those who are in the Lord Jesus Christ from eternity to eternity.'

It is most instructive to see how Paul handles a situation that could have become very negative. Any time we deal with human beings we are going to have some negatives. If you went to a perfect church, once you got there, it would no longer be perfect. So you can be certain there will be problems, and it is well to know how to face some of the criticisms. People feel more free than ever to give the fullest reign to their dislikes and their criticisms of the leadership. So how does Paul deal with these believers who have hurt him by speaking ill of him? He does not continually dwell on the disagreement or on the hurt. He does explain his side very clearly. We have a right to do that. But then he points them to the Lord Jesus who is waiting to bless them. He says in effect, 'If we look to him together, he can heal us, forgive us and restore our unity and our joy.' The apostle deals with the congregation as loving parents might deal with wayward children, not by ignoring them or becoming cold towards them, but by seeking to restore fellowship.

The generosity of God

Thirdly, we notice *the broadness of the blessing Paul points to*: 'For no matter how many promises God has made, they are "Yes" in Christ. And so through him the "Amen" is spoken by us to the glory of God' (1:20). That is the broadest field of blessing you could possibly think of. If you belong to Christ then God will take anything in the Bible from Genesis to Revelation and he will make over those promises to you as you need them, according to his knowledge of what is for his glory and for your good. It is as if you went to the bank and gave in a cheque. They would not cash it if it were not signed. With all of our needs we might feel that the cheque will bounce because we are sinful and inadequate. How do we know God will be gracious to us? But the cheque does not have your name on it. It is not dependent on your resources. The cheque is signed by the Lord Jesus Christ in his blood.

Regarding this seemingly reckless statement of Paul, John Owen says in his great book *Death of Death and the Death of Christ* that the 'Amen' is speaking of the covenant which is confirmed, ratified, unchangeably established and irrevocably made over to us. He says it was done in Christ, in his death and blood-shedding for the confirmation of the testament where all these promises are the conveyance of a legacy, as if somebody died and left you money. It is a legacy to us, confirmed by the death of the testator that made the will, as Hebrews 9:16 says. Owen goes on to say that it is a summary of all the promises of God in the covenant of grace. Everything you could ever need is included in this, from your birth to your standing in glorified perfection before God. He speaks of God's promise in Jeremiah 31:33-34 to give us new hearts in which his law is written so that we follow him and we know his guidance.

Someone may ask, 'How can I know how God will guide me?' Every time you say 'Amen' in Christ, the guidance is there because it is made over to you. He says all that we need in justification, in sanctification, in the hour of our death, is made over to us in the

Lord Jesus Christ. He is God's 'Amen' to all the promises of the Bible. God is saying to you, 'Jesus Christ is my answer to your need', because God sent him to die and be raised for you, and God crucified and raised you in him. You say 'Amen' and God is also saying, 'Amen. Yes, it shall be yours.' See yourself affirmed and 'Amen-ed' in Christ. Culture becomes a wasteland when it depends on self. It springs to life when it depends on the Lord Jesus, the Life-giver.

God's plan for church growth (2:5-11)

Fourthly, Paul now shows that *those who are 'Amen-ed' by God must re-echo that 'Amen' to other people.* One of the reasons God leaves you in the world and does not take you to be with himself the minute you get saved, is that you may live and function as his 'Amen' to the general public, to your little circle, to wherever he puts you. God sends you out to be his 'Amen' to needy, unworthy, seeking souls. As Jesus says in John 20:21, 'As the Father has sent me, I am sending you.' Just think of a congregation full of people receiving the 'Amen' of the grace of God in the Lord Jesus Christ and going out with that fragrance upon them. They can be God's 'Amen' in the shop, the university, the store, on the bus, with the children they meet and wherever they are. That is one of the major modes of the church going forward in the most natural ways.

What is forgiven must be forgotten

There was a man in the Corinthian church who was a ringleader in trouble-making and had grievously offended Paul. He tried to split the church, and he was the one who necessitated Paul's painful visit. But the church dealt with this man according to biblical discipline. He was censured and chastised; as a result he really repented and was gloriously changed. Yet there were some people in Corinth who wanted to stay angry with him. The apostle Paul is saying to the good people at Corinth, 'Don't stay angry with this man. He has repented. Be God's "Amen" to him. Receive him. Take him back in. Love him as God loves you. Echo God's "Amen" to this man who was troublesome but has changed his behaviour.'

There is a great deal of evil in a community where grudges are held against those who have repented, just as in a family one of the worst things someone can do is to drag up things that a wife or a husband or a child did years ago. The wrongdoer has apologised. It should have been forgotten and put behind. What a terrible thing it is to drag up something wrong a person did and hold it before them. That is the opposite of the way we 'Amen' a person. That is to negate them. In God's family we do not speak of past faults that have been put behind and we do not stay sullen.

Amidst the selfishness of the secularised and humanistic world, one of the greatest things a true church can do is be a place where true forgiveness is practised and where the unworthy are welcome to come in. As they repent and turn to Jesus, begin to come under his yoke and to learn of him, we never bring up the sordidness of things that they have done, or even speak to others about that. What a powerful testimony we have – that pagans can know they can be totally forgiven and taken in as God's dear children. In verse 11 Paul says that if we refuse to forgive, then the devil will have an entry. If you want to give an open door for the devil into your marriage or into your relationship with your children or grandchildren, or into a congregation, be hesitant and slow to forgive, hold things against people, be embittered, touchy and testy, be a bit cold to somebody who did you wrong but has apologised. Then you are opening the door wide open for the devil to come in and wreak his havoc. Hebrews 12:15 says, 'See to it that... no bitter root grows up to cause trouble and defile many.' If you want to drive the devil out, forgive, forget and ask God to give you the grace to love and go forward. That spirit is at the basis of spiritual and cultural renewal.

The divine seal of ownership

Fifthly, *Paul shows from where the power comes* to hear God's 'Amen' to my soul and to speak God's 'Amen' to those so desperately needing to hear it all around me. 'Now it is God who makes both us and you stand firm in Christ. He anointed us, set his seal of ownership on us, and put his Spirit in our hearts as a deposit, guaranteeing what is to come' (1:21-22). Paul is saying that this knowledge is one of the ways that we are given the practical power and the ability to live in the realm of grace. We have the assurance that God has established us in the eternal covenant, that he will take us through the dark waters of death victorious and he will glorify us. Because God has been gracious to us beyond our deserving, we have the ability to be kind, loving and gracious to other people beyond their deserving.

One of the ways we can be God's 'Amen' to others, as well as hear God's 'Amen' to our souls, is on the basis of what he has done for us in the Holy Spirit. He has sealed us in the Holy Spirit and given us the down payment of the Spirit in our hearts. This is spoken of in Ephesians 1:13-14: 'And you also were included in Christ when you heard the word of truth, the gospel of your salvation. Having believed, you were marked in him with a seal, the promised Holy Spirit, who is a deposit guaranteeing our inheritance until the redemption of those who are God's possession – to the praise of his glory.' I think the original text implies that the sealing of the Spirit is part of the gift of regeneration, not necessarily something that occurs later. Yes, it may develop and there may be fuller experiences, but this sealing of the Spirit, this down payment or deposit, comes with the new birth. If you were buying a house for, say, £100,000, then you would probably have to put down a deposit of, say, £5,000. The Holy Spirit is in a sense part of the fullness of what God is going to give you when you see him face to face and you are glorified. The thing that helps you know you have received the reality, not just a theory, is that the Holy Spirit comes with all the Father's love, power, grace, joy, glory and light from heaven and implants it like a seed within you. Not all of it yet, but enough for you to know it is real and true, and that you will get the rest later.

This has been the thing that has made the people of God different, and has made the church victorious in an evil generation. I am aware of the evil of the times, but I will not wring my hands over it very much because I know the resurrection power of Christ is greater than all the wickedness, filth, idolatry and evil of this decaying culture. He can turn it around just like that. All the power is there in seed-form, the down payment of the Spirit to all who belong to the Lord. If we began to enter into the joy and into the reality of that and to hear God's 'Amen' to us and be his 'Amen' to others, there is no telling how rapidly we could see a change all across our secularised, burned-out, cynical countries.

In the 1730s the young Jonathan Edwards, one of the great men of faith, lived in New England. He describes in his memoirs, entitled *Resolutions*, how he entered more into what he already had in the down payment of the Spirit:

> After this, my sense of divine things gradually increased and became more and more lively and had more of that inward sweetness. The appearance of everything was altered. There seemed to be, as it were, a calm, sweet cast or appearance of divine glory in almost every thing. God's excellency, His wisdom, His purity and love seemed to appear in everything. In the sun, moon and stars, in the cloud and blue sky, in the grass, flowers, trees, in the water and all nature which used greatly to fix my mind. I often used to sit and view the moon for a long time and in the day, spent much time in viewing the clouds and sky to behold the sweet glory of God in these things, in the meantime, singing forth with a low voice my contemplations of the creator and redeemer. I felt a burning desire to be, in everything, a complete Christian and conformed to the blessed image of Christ. It was my continual strife day and night how I should be more holy and live more holily and more becoming

a child of God and a disciple of Christ. The heaven I desired was the heaven of holiness – to be with God and to spend my eternity in divine love and holy communion with Christ. My mind was very much taken up with contemplations on heaven and the enjoyments there and living there in perfect holiness, humility and love and it used to appear at that time a great part of the happiness of heaven that there the saints could express their love to Christ. My heart panted after this – to lie low before God as in the dust that I might be nothing and that God might be all, that I might become as a little child.

The late Duncan Campbell speaks of a similar experience in the Lewis revival in the Hebrides in the late 1940s and early 50s:

> Revival is God let loose through human personality, and there you have the flood-gates of heaven opened and the dry places flooded with God. Revival is a community saturated with God. Men move on to their Christless hell but when God steps down, when hearts are made clean by Him, then He finds an avenue through which He can move and the community becomes saturated with God so that many of those who find the Saviour come into saving relationship with Him before they come near any church or place of meeting.

I believe the apostle Paul is teaching us that the inheritance we have, the down payment of the blessed Holy Spirit that every true child of God has in his regeneration, is more than sufficient to enable us to have the supernatural reality of walking in the Spirit. As we yield to God and seek his face in his Word, we walk in the light, cleansed in the blood of the Lord Jesus, so that we may live on the basis of God 'Amen-ing' us in Christ, and go forth to be God's 'Amen' to those who need him so very much in our secular culture. God help us to hear the 'Amen' and to be that very 'Amen' until we sing that word of grace around the throne in glory.

4

God's Reality in the Face of Cultural Superficiality

2 Cor 2:12-17

[12]Now when I went to Troas to preach the gospel of Christ and found that the Lord had opened a door for me, [13]I still had no peace of mind, because I did not find my brother Titus there. So I said good-bye to them and went on to Macedonia.

[14]But thanks be to God, who always leads us in triumphal procession in Christ and through us spreads everywhere the fragrance of the knowledge of him. [15]For we are to God the aroma of Christ among those who are being saved and those who are perishing. [16]To the one we are the smell of death; to the other, the fragrance of life. And who is equal to such a task? [17]Unlike so many, we do not peddle the word of God for profit. On the contrary, in Christ we speak before God with sincerity, like men sent from God.

A friend from California, who has a good sense of humour, once gave my wife an apron with these words embroidered on it: 'Before truth, the right fork.' It was a way of making fun of the widespread attitude which puts style above substance and elegance above character.

One of the things that goes with an increasing secularism is a tendency to be impressed by the immediate, the powerful and the superficial; great emphasis is laid on what is both outwardly attractive and pragmatically effective. The reason is that secularism has denied the transcendent reality of God and the spiritual world. In the midst of a materialistic culture, even God's church can begin to adopt the values of the secular world, believing that what brings in numbers of people and money immediately is of first-rank importance. If your methodology is not 'successful' in this sense then it has to be shifted; perhaps even your message must be changed to achieve results and win influence. 2 Corinthians 2:12-17 certainly gives us an approach to gospel ministry very different from the one that we get from the secular mentality that has affected the church.

In Zechariah 4:10 the prophet raises a significant question in this regard: 'Who despises the day of small things?' In Matthew 13:33 Jesus tells a parable of the kingdom of heaven in terms of a woman who hid a small portion of yeast in a large amount of flour. Although quite unnoticed and apparently insignificant to the eyes of observers, it leavened the whole loaf. It made all the difference, causing it to rise, giving it shape and making it what it was. That is how a valid Christian ministry is working in most cases.

This hymn by FW Faber from the Church of Scotland Hymnary expresses the hiddenness of God's work:

Workman of God! O lose not heart,
But learn what God is like,
And, in the darkest battle-field,
Thou shalt know where to strike.

Thrice blest is he to whom is given
The instinct that can tell
That God is on the field when He
Is most invisible.

He hides himself so wondrously,
As though there were no God;
He is least seen when all the powers
Of ill are most abroad.

The pastor's heart (2:12-17)

The first thing we must notice is *a minister's heart burdened by his work.* He has given his very soul to these people, but he is weighed down by the seeming insignificance, or lack of success, of a work into which he had so poured his energies. He is speaking of his visit to Troas when he had an opportunity to preach. He found it next to impossible to do it, as he was so torn with grief over the situation with the Corinthian Christians (v. 13). He had written them a painful letter, then made a visit but had to withdraw. We read in another place that he had hoped that Titus would come and bring him word that the measures he had taken with this congregation he loved so dearly had accomplished what was intended. Yet Titus had not come, and the situation was apparently so distressing to Paul that he was not able to take advantage of the opportunity at Troas. This could be connected to verse 8 of chapter 1: 'We do not want you to be uninformed, brothers, about the hardships we suffered in the province of Asia. We were under great pressure, far beyond our ability to endure, so that we despaired even of life.' Then he goes on to speak of the blessing arising even out of that situation.

One thing we can certainly say about Paul, burdened down as he was at that time over the Corinthians, is that he was far from being a detached observer. I remember a number of years ago hearing a man say to a group of younger ministers something like this, 'Now, if you go into a ministry and you want to preserve your mental and physical health and have a successful family life and be a good husband and father, and also you would like to get somewhere in the ministry, essentially you must be professionally disengaged from the people. Do not let them get at you. Keep people at a certain arm's length so that your emotions cannot pull you down. Be a religious professional.' All sorts of reasons were given to make it sound spiritual, but the essence was that emotional detachment must be cultivated. On this basis the apostle Paul would certainly have failed his course!

C S Lewis has a moving passage in his book *The Four Loves* where he says that if you want to preserve your mental composure and your emotional well-being as a person, then do not get into a love-relationship with anybody – a wife, a child, or even a dog or cat. He says, 'Love someone and your heart will be wrung and possibly broken.' So to be professional and disengaged in the ministry, you must not give your heart, you must not begin to love. Lewis goes on to say in a rather intriguing fashion, 'What you can do is wrap your heart up in little luxuries, in hobbies and, as it were, put it in a golden coffin, but in the coffin it changes and becomes essentially unbreakable and irredeemable.' One has seen ministers who have maybe been hurt and started protecting themselves this way, by wrapping themselves up, insulating and isolating themselves. Paul did not protect himself in that way and thus he had a heart that was deeply burdened over the Corinthians.

Water into wine

Secondly, we notice *a minister's heart lifted up*; in moving from verses 12-13 to verse 14, it feels as if Paul has suddenly experienced God's spotlight shining on his situation and giving him understanding. We read elsewhere that the reason he has this sudden burst of joy and begins speaking of the triumph in Christ, is that Titus reached him with news that the Corinthians had wonderfully accepted the rebukes of Paul, and the Holy Spirit had been at work. The experience of ministering to this very difficult, often self-centred, proud congregation, was really like the water turning into wine. Now he knows it was worth the uncertainty and the worry and the feeling of powerlessness. He realises God has been at work and the Lord Jesus has triumphed. If verses 12-13 represent a woman in the pains of labour, then verse 14 celebrates the healthy birth of a beautiful child.

The hidden pattern of faithful ministry

Thirdly, we notice in verses 14-16 *a hidden pattern behind the downs and the ups of a faithful Christian ministry*. It is as if the Lord all unseen is walking in the midst of the candlesticks of a ministry of word and sacrament and prayer. In the necessary downs and ups, an invisible presence is working a pattern of great meaning and importance that most of the time we do not see, at least not for a good while. At times our culture seems to despise our ministry and message, and we feel buried under much dirt, but something essential is going on. The 'being buried' is just as essential as what follows it.

Paul uses an illustration in terms of a Roman military parade to help us discern this invisible pattern that gives meaning to all our efforts. When a very successful army general would come back to Rome, he would be given a great parade and accorded almost literally divine honours in the later Empire. The whole city would turn out in tens of thousands lining the streets and throwing flowers as he passed by. In his triumphal train he would have his captives dressed up in their native costumes to show that he had won impressive spoils for the great Roman Empire. The carvings on the arch of Titus in Rome depict native Jews being led captive in chains in a triumphal procession, spreading the incense associated with divine honours.

Paul says that is what it is like with the Christian ministry. Sometimes we feel as if we are in chains because there are very definite constraints and restraints in our lives if we are bound to the

Lord Jesus. Sometimes we may feel as if we are being dragged along faster than we can walk. There is a brokenness that may not feel much like triumph when we are in the chains, but when we look back at our life and ministry in the light of who Jesus Christ is and what he is doing, then we can see the whole picture. Paul realises that when he was the most burdened over Corinth, even unable to preach at Troas, that he was being led by Christ in his own triumphal procession through a pagan world. What was happening to Paul in his very brokenness was in some way being supernaturally used to spread the fragrance of the beauty of the Lord Jesus. Paul's constraint was a door through which the Lord's resurrection power was reaching his generation as they, as it were, watched the parade go by. Every Christian ministry that is faithful to the truth is like this, little though it feels like it. We feel the chains and we usually do not smell the incense or the flowers.

Paul then speaks of a sweet perfume in verse 15: 'For we are to God the aroma of Christ among those who are being saved and those who are perishing.' It is impossible to attempt to follow Jesus Christ and to preach the Word, without a fragrance going out from your life. It is, of course, the Holy Spirit who is the perfume of God's people. With God helping us we are able to preach the truth in the power of the Holy Spirit; we proclaim what the Word of God says, and seek to be conformed to it ourselves. It is the Holy Spirit who spreads out the sweet fragrance which the human heart is made to desire. Through the Fall we lost the taste of it at the gates of the Garden of Eden. Adam hid from God and our generation still hides from him; humanity cannot taste the sweetness of fellowship with God, yet we are made for him so that we long for that sweetness. Paul wrote in Romans 5:11 that 'we also rejoice in God' because of what the Lord Jesus has done for his people as a propitiation. The God-man stands between us reconciling God to human beings so that we can taste the divine sweetness. This hymn well expresses the sweetness:

Loved with everlasting love,
Led by grace that love to know;
Spirit, breathing from above,
Thou hast taught me it is so.
O this full and perfect peace!
O this transport all divine!
In a love that cannot cease
I am His, and He is mine.

Heaven above is softer blue,
Earth around is sweeter green;
Something lives in every hue,
Christless eyes have ever seen:
Birds with gladder songs o'erflow,
Flowers with deeper beauties shine,
Since I know, as now I know,
I am His, and He is mine.

The revolt against the gospel

We notice, however, something else that the apostle says here very realistically: this same sweet fragrance smells like the most awful stench imaginable to those who are rejecting the gospel. We need to understand how the gospel of the Lord Jesus Christ affects the person who insists on living for self and tramples underfoot the worthy blood of Christ. Usually it is wise not to take people's rejection of our message quite so personally, because we realise what a threat the preaching of the love of the Lord Jesus is to the secular mind. It is not that one fragrance goes out to the elect and another fragrance goes out to the reprobate. It is the same gospel and the same message. We should not be discouraged because of the hostility that it provokes, for the power of the resurrection of Christ is able still to transform our Western, jaded, post-modern, secular culture. Nevertheless, we have to be prepared for much of the anti-Christianity that we see.

In the United States, it is surprising how some of the organisations of secularist lawyers and other groups are working to take down the Ten Commandments out of courthouses and schools. There may have been a copy of the Scripture verses engraved in marble within these institutions for two hundred years, yet now some of these secular groups are saying that to impose religion upon free people is an intrusion on their rights. We may wonder how an intelligent person can think this way when the ethos of the country is based on these Scriptures, but we need to understand that any memorial of God is a horror to the secular mind.

I was once invited to preach in a liberal church, and as I spoke on the early verses of 1 Corinthians 15 a woman in the congregation literally vomited as a result. In another incident in a different church, I was preaching on the second commandment explaining why Presbyterian worship had traditionally been simple. I did not think I had said anything that would have been offensive to a person from another tradition, but one lady was evidently infuriated. She said, 'I'll never set foot in that awful church again with such a prejudiced, narrow-minded, terrible minister. I was offended and personally attacked.' But she got so worried that she started reading her Bible, and as she read Romans chapter 8, God saved her, and from then on she never missed a service! After that it worried me a little less when people got angry with me. Do not worry about the psychological effect of the gospel and do not try to alter its smell; God is in charge of that and he will take care of it.

Seeker-friendly services

The church growth movement in the USA has a tendency to advocate that ministers who want their churches to grow should develop what are called 'seeker-friendly services'. Some would advocate we should purposely work to remove things that would be offensive to a secular man or woman so that in some way we can get them in, entertain them and in a sense claim success. In other words, remove the offensive smell and then you can grow a church. If you remove the smell of the gospel – the sin, the hell – you are also going to remove the sweetness of the gospel – the forgiveness, the eternal pardon, the unspeakable glory, the bliss of the redeemed. Changing the smell to water down the offensiveness of the truth of God also changes the sweetness, because there is a sense in which the gospel is antagonistic to human nature (1 Cor. 1:18).

'Who is equal to such a task?'

Fourthly, Paul asks the question at the end of verse 16, *'Who is equal to such a task?'* Who has the strength to minister in a secular culture that rejects the pure truth of God? It is easy to suggest that we should be brave and broken and willing to make costly sacrifices, but it is a lot harder to practise it. How can we live in such a way that Jesus Christ triumphs, given our own weakness, given our own tendency to protect ourselves and given the viciousness of the time in which we live? Who is sufficient for the ups and the downs of a real ministry? Who is able to preach and live this gospel so that the Lord Jesus is seen, the fragrance goes out, the lost are redeemed and thus come to love the God they used to hate?

Paul answers his question here by saying that we can make it if we receive and then give out God's Word – straight, entire and pure. We need to submit to the patterns of the very thing we are seeking to give out to others. Robert Murray McCheyne used to emphasise that all ministers needed to pray, 'Lord, do in me first what I am asking you to do in this congregation. Apply the preaching to my life that I am seeking to have applied to this people whom you have given me.' So when we take God's Word, even when its challenges make us uncomfortable, and then give it out straight and pure, God's sufficiency in the blessed Holy Spirit will be there to make the fragrance go out to accomplish Christ's purposes.

The teacher's temptation

We have a natural tendency because we are human beings, not because we are hypocrites or evil, demonic persons, but just because we are not yet living in sinless perfection, to water down God's Word one way or another. The truest minister will face the temptation to hold back parts of it in order to get a better psychological reaction, although we like to call it a spiritual response; we say that these people respond better if you do not speak of hell. Some of the church-growth teachers are saying that you must not speak of the negative. Two ministers who attended a church growth seminar were told that they must not be controversial in their preaching. Don't deal with big issues that would divide people as, for instance, abortion or homosexuality. Statistics showed if you dealt with those things, even on the basis of a biblical text, that you could offend and drive away part of your people and the church couldn't grow as much if you dealt with those negative, divisive issues. Deal with things that help people face life, be successful, be better-integrated personalities.

Now, of course, one accepts the point that we are not in the pulpit to preach partisan politics and that we are not to be nasty, mean-spirited preachers, always lambasting sin in a censorious spirit. But when the Word of God is clearly teaching things that a particular generation does not want to receive, dare we hold back from declaring such things if they come on God's authority? After all, as Paul says in 2 Corinthians 5:20, we are Christ's ambassadors. An ambassador has a received message which he is not at liberty to change; if he did so he would be a traitor. We are not in a position to change the message to get a better reaction.

James Denney in his great commentary on 2 Corinthians speaks of verse 17 where the apostle is using an expression translated in the Authorised Version as the word 'corrupt' (NIV 'peddle the word of God'). He says that in ancient days this term was applied in tavern-keeping to all the devices by which the wine sellers deceived their customers. Basically it was the idea of blending and adulterating, so that by putting in more water and diluting the wine, you could make more money.

There are two separate strands here in the idea of corrupting the Word of God. One is that of men qualifying the gospel, infiltrating their own ideas into the Word of God, tempering its severity or perhaps its goodness, veiling its inexorableness in order to compromise its straightness. The other idea is that all such proceedings are faithless and dishonest because some private interest underlies them. It need not be avarice, though it may be. Ministers may corrupt the Word of God, making it the stock-in-trade of a paltry business of their own, in many other ways than by subordinating it to the need of a livelihood. When they exercise their calling as ministers for the gratification of their vanity, they do exactly this. When they preach not to draw attention to what God says, but rather to emphasise their own cleverness, learning, humour, fine voice or gestures, they do this. They make the Word minister to themselves rather than being ministers of the Word – that is, they themselves, instead of the Lord Jesus, are leading the triumphal procession.

James Denney goes on to say that the key word is 'sincerity', derived from the Latin *sine cere*, meaning 'without wax'. This refers to the practice of using wax to hide a break in a piece of marble in order to sell it dishonestly. By contrast, sincerity is a solid, real thing without any pretence. The pure and full Word received into my life and given out in my ministry, regardless of my assessment of the reactions it may cause, always goes along with the personal presence of the risen, crucified Lord Jesus Christ. That is the price and that is the gain of such a ministry.

Corrupting the Word of God

One trainee minister I know went for an interview to a church where the minister said to him, 'If you came here would you be willing to go along with seeker-oriented services?' The trainee asked what was involved, and was told that the services are set up in such a way that the unchurched will feel happy to come. They will not feel out of place or awkward and will find it very friendly, not demanding too much of them at first. But then the trainee was told, 'If you came here it would never do to preach on sin on Sunday morning – that could turn off a seeker and not be friendly.' The trainee replied, 'You don't want me to preach on sin? What do you want me to preach on?' He was told, 'We have special meetings for the Christians during the week; you can tell them about it at those meetings. But I don't want to have a negative attitude in this church. We're trying to grow. We're near a major university. What would the university people think if we preached on sin on Sunday morning?' The trainee pointed out that some of them might get saved, but that was the end of the interview. In my view such an attitude towards preaching represents a direct corruption of the Word of God. This is what Paul is saying we must not do, if we want the fragrance of Jesus.

Statistics in the USA show that you can get a pretty big crowd into church if you are clever enough at entertaining. But what is the point of having warm, breathing bodies if they are not regenerate? They miss the sweetness and fragrance as well as the offensiveness of the same true gospel, and they are not coming into contact with the Lord Jesus Christ. I am not saying that all the mega-churches are corrupting the Word of God; no doubt we can learn things from some of them, but we do not go by what is superficially impressive and seems to give improved quarterly earnings and immediate effects. We all like results, but what we have to remember is that faithfulness to Christ is like the yeast hidden in the flour. Let us not despise the day of small things. Much of a faithful ministry takes time and can seem like small things in any generation. If the ministry is of God it will have the fragrance of the true gospel – the whole Word given out by a man who is submitted to it, sometimes broken by it but always resurrected by it. That will win the day, and we will know as we look back that the Lord Jesus is in this, and that he is leading us in triumph.

Christ's train of triumph

We remember how Elisha and his servant were surrounded by the hostile army of the king of Syria, who knew that Elisha was thwarting his military plans, and was determined to kill him (2 Kings 6:14-17). When the servant saw this large army with its weapons he was terrified, but Elisha prayed for him that God would open his eyes to see the spiritual reality of the unseen army of the Lord all around them. It is not our business to see into the invisible world because Scripture is given to us as sufficient. If, however, we could see the invisible company of angels around us, we would realise that the powerful, infinitely wise providence of God is working on behalf of all those who belong to Christ and have his interests at heart. Even in our darkest nights when we receive the most unfair criticism, we would be aware that 'those who are with us are more than those who are with them'. While the seed of wheat that falls into the ground is buried and dying, and the day seems one of small things, we can trust God until the morning. Then we will look back and see that we were led in the train of the triumph of Christ, who alone can make us equal to such a task.

It is the reality of Christ's triumphant presence operating deep within the yielded Christian life that does indeed yield a true elegance and propriety of style to the plainest believer. But 'the right fork' (if by that we mean considerateness of spirit and dignity of personal bearing) flows only out of a life hidden with Christ in God. This 'right fork' comes after truth, not before it. It is nothing less than a foreshadowing of some of the beauteous characteristics of resurrection morning. It is available only to those who are real with the risen Christ, and who cut through all external pretence that others may be real with him.

5

Resurrection Now

2 Cor 3

[1]*Are we beginning to commend ourselves again? Or do we need,*
like some people, letters of recommendation to you or from you? [2]*You*
yourselves are our letter, written on our hearts, known and read by
everybody. [3]*You show that you are a letter from Christ, the result of*
our ministry, written not with ink but with the Spirit of the living
God, not on tablets of stone but on tablets of human hearts.

[4]*Such confidence as this is ours through Christ before God.* [5]*Not*
that we are competent in ourselves to claim anything for ourselves,
but our competence comes from God. [6]*He has made us competent as*
ministers of a new covenant—not of the letter but of the Spirit; for
the letter kills, but the Spirit gives life.

[7]*Now if the ministry that brought death, which was engraved in*
letters on stone, came with glory, so that the Israelites could not look
steadily at the face of Moses because of its glory, fading though it
was, [8]*will not the ministry of the Spirit be even more glorious?* [9]*If the*
ministry that condemns men is glorious, how much more glorious is
the ministry that brings righteousness! [10]*For what was glorious has*

> *no glory now in comparison with the surpassing glory.* [11]*And if what*
> *was fading away came with glory, how much greater is the glory of*
> *that which lasts!*
>
> [12]*Therefore, since we have such a hope, we are very bold.* [13]*We are*
> *not like Moses, who would put a veil over his face to keep the Israel-*
> *ites from gazing at it while the radiance was fading away.* [14]*But their*
> *minds were made dull, for to this day the same veil remains when the*
> *old covenant is read. It has not been removed, because only in Christ*
> *is it taken away.* [15]*Even to this day when Moses is read, a veil covers*
> *their hearts.* [16]*But whenever anyone turns to the Lord, the veil is*
> *taken away.* [17]*Now the Lord is the Spirit, and where the Spirit of the*
> *Lord is, there is freedom.* [18]*And we, who with unveiled faces all reflect*
> *the Lord's glory, are being transformed into his likeness with ever-*
> *increasing glory, which comes from the Lord, who is the Spirit.*

What good news that we do not have to wait till the end of time to experience the reality of resurrection power within us and around us! Much in chapter 2 has been about the deaths to be died in the Christian ministry, but in chapter 3 we begin to see some of the resurrections that inevitably attend the faithful living and the preaching of the Word of God in the power of the blessed Holy Spirit.

So very much is being said in Western Europe and the USA about the change in our culture that some ministers seem to be responding in panic, by altering the message to reach the secularist. Yet when we read the Church Fathers writing in the first four hundred years that the gospel went out, the culture of the ancient Greek and Roman world was every bit as secular as modern Western culture, if not worse. There was paganism, relativism, immorality, unbelief, violence, cruelty and social disintegration then as now. So I do not see our present age as a time for wringing our hands in despair or panicking over what we should do next. It is very clear from 2 Corinthians 2:17 that the answer is always the same truth. Of course we have to speak it in a way that it can be understood, dealing with the questions of the time, but it is always the same pattern of truth lived out in the same Holy Spirit.

What 2 Corinthians 3 is talking about is what won the rotting, collapsing Roman Empire to the Lord Jesus Christ. It was the glorious effectiveness of the gospel ministry through imperfect human beings in a culture in which most of the intellectuals rejected the very possibility of absolute truth. But it was the glory of the lives of the Christians that was such a profound argument for who the Lord Jesus is, so that when everything else was falling apart, even the pagans turned to the Christians. One of the Christian writers named Origen wrote a book against paganism entitled *Contra Celsum*, in which he makes this moving statement:

> Everywhere I go, Christ is spoken against by the leaders and what Christ stands for is considered a threat to the government and to the other religions, and yet the glory of Jesus Christ is shining in the lives of ordinary men and women all through this Empire and numbers are every day being converted because they see the glory of Jesus in the flesh and the blood of ordinary men and women.

However secular a situation is, however much the universities or the media say there is no possibility of knowing absolute truth, when you have a Daniel, when you have a Job, when you have just an ordinary Christian walking in the light, walking in the Spirit, loving Christ, faithfully serving God, ministering his truth as best they can, there is a glory that breaks forth. That is the most powerful argument which can break hearts and open doors. It can change everything all around. It is an irresistible power which can change everything, and this is what the apostle is talking about in 2 Corinthians 3.

Effective ministry (3:1-3)

The first three verses of chapter 3 deal with the effectiveness of the Christian ministry, while verses 4-18 focus on the glory of that ministry. First, let us consider *its effectiveness*. In the nineteenth century the famous Baptist preacher, Spurgeon, was approached by a young college student who was discouraged by the lack of results from his preaching. Spurgeon, who was a man known to tease students and others, looked at him and said, 'Well, young man, you certainly don't expect people to be converted every time you preach, do you?' The young man said, 'Of course not!' Spurgeon said, 'Well, that's your problem.'

The apostle Paul is saying that in the good providence of God, true Christian ministration of his Word backed by prayer will ultimately have an effectiveness that will be accredited. Such a ministry will hold the Word pure and entire, and will live it out in a holy life which will not be perfect but will in sincerity look to Jesus Christ.

How is the Christian ministry accredited? Generally, any new theological college, university or school would be subject to authorities called accrediting agencies that would come in and see if things were being done properly. But the picture here is different. The apostle says that his accreditation as an effective minister (a word meaning 'servant' or 'slave') of Jesus Christ is the lives of men and women in Corinth. These were the people who had given Paul so much trouble and yet he is saying that Christ is in them and they are his accreditation; the effectiveness of his Christian ministry is seen in the lives of the people who sit under that ministry. It is not that some agency writes a letter of recommendation or accreditation of this institution. The apostle says that Christian ministry is accredited not by ink on paper, but by the Holy Spirit drawing the lineaments of the character of the Lord Jesus Christ in the responses of the men and the women who give themselves to the pattern of Christian truth that is proclaimed.

Beautiful 'letters'

There is a wonderful saying in Latin on the tomb of Sir Christopher Wren in the crypt of St Paul's Cathedral in London, which translates into English, 'If you require a monument, look around you.' Wren was the architect of St Paul's and of many other marvellous churches and buildings in London and Cambridge. He is saying, 'If you want a memorial of my life, of my work, what I stood for, what I amounted to, walk around this cathedral. This is my monument. I just happen to be buried in it.' If you want a monument of a Christian minister, it is not so important to go to the graveyard where he is buried, but to look at the lives of the people that sat under his ministry. They are the 'letters' showing that God used him – the Holy Spirit did it really – but God used him to write those 'letters'. A true minister, of course, is always concerned, not merely for the regeneration of souls, but also for the sanctification, for the development, for the beautifying of those 'letters'. Ultimately that is what gives the Christian ministry its effectiveness. Even the secularist cannot argue away a changed life, a life of love, a life that is unselfish, a marriage that is pure, children that are raised rightly; their witness breaks down all kinds of prejudices and arguments against the truth of God.

Some of the most faithful preaching I have ever heard was from an American Indian minister who, if he heard that one of his congregation had not paid a bill, would go and pay it for them, though he was not a rich man. He wanted to protect the reputation of that congregation in the community. Like the apostle Paul, he did not want anybody upon whom he was seeking to write the character of Christ, to owe a penny past the time that it should have been paid. One of the most important means of evangelism is the lives of the people of God having their responses changed by the life of the Lord Jesus written upon them so that they are breathing and manifesting the atmosphere of a different world.

Statistics from the Billy Graham Association indicate that over 90 percent of all the people who came forward at their crusades said they had seen some person who was living a Christian life that impressed them. They had seen either in their work, school or neighbourhood somebody whose life revealed a different world which was beginning to break open their selfishness and their secularism. It made them question whether there is not something else, something better or higher. Then when they heard the Christian message they were evidently prepared to make some sort of response to it.

The Christian ministry's effectiveness is that the gospel becomes translated into flesh and blood, and that has a way of beginning to transform an entire society. That is how the West became Christian. Although at present our culture has turned its back on God, it could turn back to the Lord again. The more he pours out his Spirit, the more the truth is proclaimed, there is no telling how fast it could begin turning back in a Christian direction.

I do not accept the theory of historicism, that once the pendulum begins to swing towards secularism, it can only go further in that direction. Culture was secular in Roman times, and in the late medieval times; then the Reformation came and it went back in the other direction. Given that Jesus Christ is risen and that God has his eternally predestined purposes, the pendulum could easily go back, bringing a more Christian situation than we have ever seen in our lives. I do not know what will happen, but I know that God will bless his ministry to which he calls us to be faithful.

The glory of ministry (3:4-18)

Secondly, we are thinking about *the Christian ministry's glory*, not the glory of the minister – he is just a servant – but the glory of God: 'Let your light shine before men, that they may see your good works and glorify your Father which is in heaven.' (Matt. 5 :16AV) Paul speaks about this glory of the Christian ministry in terms of covenant. Covenant is an agreement whereby he relates to us to save us and to fulfil the stipulations of who he is in saving us. The whole Bible is held together in what we call different phases of the one covenant of grace: Adam would have been able to keep the law and to fulfil the terms of the covenant, but he was disobedient and the human race became unable to live up to it, so God deals with us on the basis of his grace.

'The letter kills' (v. 6)
The apostle Paul is here contrasting two phases of this covenant of grace that run through the Bible; he is speaking of the old Mosaic covenant. It had a legal and external emphasis, although there was grace in the provision of a sacrifice for sin. But the old covenant was characterised by the demands of the law outside the heart and a certain killing work of the law – 'The letter kills' (v. 6). The law is a transcript of the character of God, showing us the holiness, purity and righteousness of God. As the law comes to us we begin to see how the purity of God would require that we treat others properly by not stealing, lying, envying and so on. Then we begin to see our darkness and how unlike God we are. Paul says it is like a killing work that makes us realise we need help.

Fading glory (v. 7)
The old covenant had a very definite glory in it. The whole mountain was shaking when the Ten Commandments were revealed to Moses, and there was a brightness about it. When Moses came down to bring the law to the people, his face was almost on fire like the bush he had originally seen. From this derives the motto of the Church of Scotland, '*Nec tamen consumebatur*' ('Nevertheless not being consumed'). Because Moses had got so near to God and because the law had so much of God's holiness and God's true character in it, the glory of the Lord was literally shining out of his face and he did not know it.

That is one of the principles of the Christian life and ministry: those who shine the most for the Lord Jesus are the least aware of it, they are looking to him rather than expecting others to look at them. The face of Moses so reflected the holy, glorious presence of God that the people asked him to cover his face with a veil so they would not be overcome by the glory. Paul also says that the glory faded, and then Moses could take the veil off. It was a way of saying that the Mosaic covenant is not the permanent one, it is preparatory.

It has a glory, but the glory is fading because something is coming that is much more wonderful and abiding. This will be a glory that will never fade and that you can approach without terror. It is so beautiful that you want it to fill you, change you and shine out from you to others.

Glory that lasts (vv. 8ff.)
This brings us to the new covenant, whereby the Lord puts his Spirit inside you. It is as if the natural person has a heart of stone as regards responding to God, but God takes away this heart of stone and puts a heart of flesh in its place. If I may speak anthropomorphically, not meaning this literally, God writes in our hearts with his own finger his own most essential characteristic of love. Jesus in Matthew 22:37-40 summarises the whole law as love: '"Love the Lord your God with all your heart and with all your soul and with all your mind." This is the first and greatest commandment and the second is like it: "Love your neighbour as yourself." All the Law and the Prophets hang on these two commandments.' In the new birth the Holy Spirit works so powerfully within the human personality that there is a change from self-centredness to a love of God and a love of other people. The Holy Spirit has brought the very love from the heart of the Father and the Son and put it inside our personality. That is what makes us Christians. That is the glory of God.

In John 1:14, 'The word became flesh and made his dwelling among us', the phrase in Greek means literally 'tabernacled'. Thus Christ represents the tabernacle and all it stood for. Then Colossians 1:27 speaks of 'Christ in you, the hope of glory.' Christ is all that the tabernacle and the temple stood for. When Solomon's temple was dedicated, the glory of the Lord came down so brightly that the priests had to come running out, so overwhelming was the sight. The glory of God came in the tabernacle and the temple, but the glory of God was most fully seen in the life, death and resurrection of the Lord Jesus Christ. The Holy Spirit comes from the Father and the Son bringing 'Christ in you, the hope of glory'; it is the glory of

God in the face of Jesus Christ, literally put inside us.

In the nineteenth century Professor Milligan of Aberdeen wrote a book on the resurrection of our Lord, in which he raised the question of why the Holy Spirit had not indwelt believers in the same powerful way before Pentecost that he had after Pentecost. He is not denying that the Holy Spirit helped believers – Psalm 51 would teach you that – but there is a difference after Pentecost. The indwelling of the glory, after Christ's death and resurrection, is in a new phase of the covenant. Professor Milligan makes an interesting suggestion (which I paraphrase):

> The glory could not come down before Jesus had made the supreme sacrifice of himself and that sacrifice had been accepted, as the Father raises his Son bodily to show his acceptance of all that Jesus did in and for our humanity. If the full glory had come upon human nature before Jesus became incarnate in order to unite our humanity to his holy life, atoning death and glorious resurrection and ascension, our naked human nature would have been blown apart by the fullness of the Holy Spirit, without the miraculous adaptation that occurs in this incarnational union.

So, as Rabbi Duncan of New College used to say, 'The dust of the earth now sits on the throne of the universe.' If God had put his glory into people before Christ had adapted our humanity in himself to receive the glory of God, it would have short-circuited human nature and destroyed it. Thus the Lord Jesus has made it possible for the very glory of God to come into men, women and children to heal and transform them, rather than destroying them.

Ever-increasing glory (v. 18)

Verse 18 is saying that the essence of the Christian ministry is to hold up the truth of who Jesus Christ is, and all the ramifications of the teaching of the Word of God. Not only teaching the Word, but living it, and submitting to its disciplines: being in the fellowship of the people of God in prayer, yielding to him, obeying sacrificially and thinking his thoughts after him. One of the reasons that God leaves us on earth is so that through our obedience people can see the Lord Jesus. A supernatural power is, in a sense, given to the people of God as they minister the truth about who Jesus Christ is. Living in a materialistic culture we are tempted to think that the non-material is not real, but the supernatural world is real as well as the natural. Verse 18 tells us that we are changed by what we gaze upon. It is intellectually, psychologically, emotionally and spiritually impossible to look at the Lord Jesus Christ in faith, when the Holy Spirit is there, and to remain the same as we are: 'we... are being transformed into his likeness with ever-increasing glory'. This is already a true foretaste of resurrection power.

Some of the prophets warned the people that when they followed empty things they became empty themselves. Even delightful, sophisticated, cultured, worldly people are in varying measures aware of the superficiality, hollowness and emptiness of their lives, and many of them try to take refuge in abuse of drink, drugs, sex or political power to fill the vacuum. If you concentrate on that which is empty you will become like it, and it will fail you in the hour of your death. If you look at the Lord Jesus and follow him, you start becoming like him and the very glory of God comes down, even though you may not be aware of it. God's glory is in on the throne in heaven, but it refuses to stay there. A hymn describes heaven thus: 'There to an ocean fullness His mercy doth expand, and glory, glory dwelleth in Immanuel's land.' Yes, it is there in all its fullness and beauty, but it comes down on those who look on Jesus Christ; others will see it and the Christian ministry will not only be vindicated as effective, but God's own glory will shine out of it. This is nothing less than an early downpayment on resurrection glory. Every Christian life and ministry goes forward on the basis of many such resurrections.

6

God's Answer to Relativism

2 Cor 4:1-6

> *1 Therefore, since through God's mercy we have this ministry, we*
> *do not lose heart. 2 Rather, we have renounced secret and shameful*
> *ways; we do not use deception, nor do we distort the word of God. On*
> *the contrary, by setting forth the truth plainly we commend ourselves*
> *to every man's conscience in the sight of God. 3 And even if our gospel*
> *is veiled, it is veiled to those who are perishing. 4 The god of this age*
> *has blinded the minds of unbelievers, so that they cannot see the*
> *light of the gospel of the glory of Christ, who is the image of God.*
> *5 For we do not preach ourselves, but Jesus Christ as Lord, and our-*
> *selves as your servants for Jesus' sake. 6 For God, who said, "Let light*
> *shine out of darkness,"[1] made his light shine in our hearts to give us*
> *the light of the knowledge of the glory of God in the face of Christ.*

How can a gospel ministry be effective in this post-modern culture which denies the very possibility of absolute truth? In answering this question, I want to refer to a transcript of a discussion between three lawyers. Two of them were Christians believing in absolute truth, the other was a pagan 'secular liberal'. These lawyers were in a major urban centre taking a vacation together while the law courts were closed for the summer. As the weather was hot they went down to the seashore, dangled their feet in the water and began a discussion.

The pagan, secularist, 'post-modernist' lawyer had been criticised by one of the Christians as he bowed his head to an antique statue of a Greek goddess, Seraphis. The Christian said, 'How can you possibly do something like that, bowing to a pagan god? You know better than that.' Then the three lawyers decided to entertain themselves by discussing the issue in the form of a legal dialogue. The pagan lawyer replied, 'You Christians are a prejudiced lot. In fact, you're dangerous; anybody who says you can know an absolute truth and that there is only one way to God is politically dangerous. We have a nation here – a very large, extended nation – that is pluralist. If one group like the Christians insist that there is only one truth, only one way to God, it will break up the country, it will put us into warring groups. The fact is you can't know final truth anyway. You can't know if there's more than one God or even if there is a God. Your whole position is quite dangerous and I'm not even sure it should be tolerated.'

The two Christian lawyers argued the gospel by appealing to what the apostle Paul said in Romans 1 and 2: that the created order speaks of a Creator, that we cannot understand the world from within it – we need an external reference point, that we have a moral conscience in us which monitors right and wrong – this points to a supreme Law-giver before whom we know we are condemned for not obeying our conscience; but the good news is that we can be freed from condemnation by Christ. The pagan lawyer says at the end of the dialogue, 'You haven't exactly answered all my questions but you've shown me that there really is one truth and I'm prepared to pray to Christ.' So we see a 'post-modernist' being converted. It is a true dialogue from the year 237 AD written by an early Christian writer named Menucius Felix, who witnessed this dialogue between three Roman lawyers at the town of Ostia.

'Post-modernism' was the cultural position when the apostle Paul was living and writing. There was denial of one truth; the certainties of Platonism, Aristotelianism and Stoicism had broken down. There was widespread cynicism among the sceptics. Cicero's *Dialogues* contain statements such as 'You cannot really know truth', or 'Who knows?' The early church had to minister the gospel in a Roman Empire, which – though outwardly very strong and very impressive – was inwardly rotting and beginning to fail. There was a culture of moral relativism, manifested in the widespread practice of abortion, infanticide and homosexuality.

Our Western culture is similar in many ways to the situation that Paul faced at Corinth, although the difference is that we have rejected a Christian heritage, whereas they were rejecting a classical, philosophical heritage. So what did Paul do? He did not panic or set up another new committee. He did not need radically to change the worship or moderate the message. He stuck to the gospel. In his second letter to the Corinthians he addresses the issue of the Christian ministry – its effectiveness, its possibilities, its difficulties, its glories – in the same sort of pluralistic and cynical culture that we face.

As Paul addresses an earlier form of what we might call a post-modernist culture, there are three things that particularly stand out in the verses we are considering in this chapter. First, in verse 1, how Paul endures the difficulties. In any true ministry, the first thing we will have is difficulty, and we will never be free from it. The apostle says that one of the important things about the Christian ministry is that we stick it out. Secondly, in verses 2-5, Paul concentrates on the gospel of Christ. Thirdly, in verse 6, he explains to us how he has the strength to endure and concentrate amidst circumstances such as stoning and imprisonment that ill repaid him for the good he was doing. But through it all, the glory of God was coming down, into the very culture that would have preferred to ignore the existence of the God of the Bible.

Endurance (v. 1)

First, in verse 1 *Paul says 'we do not lose heart'* (in the Authorised Version 'we faint not'), rather we endure or we stick it out. He is dealing with the reality of troubles and attacks that will come from time to time on anyone who will put God first. It may be an unconverted elder, or it may be a powerful family in the church that resents the gospel. It may be any number of other things that cause us to faint. There is the natural tendency in the most truly converted person to faint, to back off from the nails, to remove ourselves from the source of the heat. When we read 'We are troubled on every side, we are perplexed, persecuted, cast down, always bearing about in the body the dying of the Lord Jesus' it is easy enough to exhort other people to endure. But what about when it is I myself who am being persecuted, cast down, perplexed, feeling the dying of Jesus opening up in my personality or my body? There is always a tendency to back off when pressure comes on us in a culture that does not like to hear people say that the Lord Jesus Christ is the only truth, and that Holy Scripture is the one infallible Word. If you ever get interviewed by the media you will face this hostility, although they may be sophisticated enough to disguise it. Let us be careful how we conduct ourselves so that we avoid seeming brusque or foolish, but let us not faint in the face of criticism.

The sell-out to modernism

One of the reasons that so much of the Western Protestant church is in complete disarray is because it fainted at the beginning of the twentieth century. The theological colleges, to a large degree, sold themselves out to the thinking of secular, anti-supernaturalist modernism that powerfully influenced and dominated the academic world. These developments have been described in two interesting studies, one by Richard Riesen on George Adam Smith, Robertson Smith and A B Davidson entitled *Criticism and Faith in Late Victorian Scotland* and another by Nicholas Needham entitled *The Doctrine of Holy Scriptures in the Free Church Fathers.*

Under pressure from the rest of the academic world, Protestant scholars succumbed to the temptation to be regarded as relevant, forward-looking and worth hearing. But what do you have to say when you no longer proclaim Jesus Christ as the incarnate, crucified, risen Son of God who is the one way of truth? The church is left with a message of do-good moralism. How does that save a soul? Thankfully God has called people into the ministry who believe the historic gospel, and he has raised up smaller denominations and faithful groups within the main denominations, but we still have a great deal of ground to recover from the collapse of the church in our culture. Unless we see a major Holy Spirit revival, we are going to be ministering in an increasingly anti-Christian atmosphere in the twenty-first century, even in the more conservative parts of the world. Yet we must not faint: Galatians 6:9 exhorts us not to grow weary in doing good.

Notice the reason that Paul gives for not fainting. He does not say, 'Now I am a wonderful person; I was taken up into the heaven of heavens and I saw the Lord.' He alludes to the fact that he was taken up into heaven where he saw the Lord himself, although he does not tell us the details (12:2f.). So he has no doubt about the reality of Christianity, but that is not the reason he gives for not fainting. Presumably those of us who are in the Christian ministry have had some kind of real experience with God, but that will not keep you from fainting. Even witnessing something of a revival may not prevent you from fainting when the pressure is on you twenty years later. Paul says the reason he does not faint under the regular pressures of the ministry as well as the more dramatic incidents of shipwreck, beating, stoning, imprisonment and the possibility of execution, is that he has received mercy. It is the mercy of God continually received that enables ministers of God to stand firm against any kind of pressure through which the providence of God allows them to pass.

The risk of getting burned

In the USA the statistics from both the Methodist church and the Southern Baptist church show that ministers are now staying less than two and a half years as an average in every pastorate, because they are encountering difficulties and they are fainting. Sometimes ministers who are facing criticism in their churches have asked whether they should take the opportunity to move to another place of service, where they feel they would be appreciated. It is understandable that they should want to get away from the heat, for which of us would want to risk getting burned? But if a minister leaves a place that is difficult too soon, there are at least two negative consequences. First, such ministers have not passed the test that the providence of God was preparing them to go through, to develop their character and to make them throw themselves the more thoroughly upon his mercy because they have come to an end of their own resources. Secondly, the church needs some heat and ministers are God's agents to make them feel it. Not in the sense of being difficult or unpleasant persons, but just in the most tender love proclaiming the gospel which causes many people to feel uneasy and to want rid of them. If a minister takes their hint and goes, the heat is removed from them, they do not get purged or shaped, and they only make it worse on the next minister. If ministers leave too soon, just as the heat was coming on and go to another place that seems easier, the test at that place will be worse, in God's providence, than the one they would have gone through if they had stayed. But we *can* stay because the mercy of God is available. However much the culture is changing or the pressure comes upon us for believing the one truth, it is no time to faint or panic. With the apostle Paul, we need to look to God and continue receiving his mercy.

Sustained by mercy

Paul's whole experience was one of receiving the mercy of God. In his original conversion, the Lord Jesus Christ seems to leave his ascended glory to come down and ask, 'Saul, Saul, why do you persecute me?' The Lord extends his pardoning love to this man, the scales fall from off his eyes and he is called to be the apostle to the Gentiles. He received mercy both in his conversion and his calling to a ministry. In Acts 18, when he was thinking about leaving a place, the Lord sends a special message to him saying in effect, 'Paul, I have many people in this city. You stay here. You do not see it right now but I have many elect. They look like goats instead of sheep, but you stay here and you continue exercising this ministry even when it is difficult, even when they put you in jail and throw you out of the synagogue. You keep on because the elect are here, the sheep are here, and if you will stay, I am going to extend you all the mercy you need and they will be gathered in and my glory will follow.'

Paul kept receiving mercy and this is how he kept going. He was in more than one shipwreck, but we are only told about one of them in Acts 27, when the storm had gone on for so long that everybody was despairing of life. But the mercy of God came in the form of an angel who told Paul that the Lord had given him the life of every man on the ship; not one would be drowned but they all must stay on the ship. So the apostle kept receiving the mercy of God, the presence of God and the sense that the sovereign God is in control, using even these circumstances to touch his elect and bring down glory. Paul kept looking up and receiving this mercy and his ministry never collapsed. Thus he was effective no matter how hostile and sceptical the culture in which he ministered.

The gospel of Christ (vv. 2-5)

Secondly, in verses 2-5 *Paul concentrates on the gospel of Christ and the ministry to which God has called him*. He concentrates on the one thing necessary by laying aside something else. The curse of many ministries today is the expectation that the minister will be able to be a businessman and administrator and fill all sorts of other roles. In many evangelical churches, the devil uses fairly good things to prevent a minister from doing the most important good thing and the essential thing. Ministries tend to go astray not so much by openly wicked temptations, although that is always possible, but often by using respectable things to keep us from the one thing necessary.

The strongest of thrills!

There are also wrong things to be renounced, as Paul tells us in verse 2. There is nothing better we can do for confused modernists, than to renounce what is wrong and to let them know where we stand if something is wrong. I once met a lady who had been brought up in the Christian Science movement, but had been converted when a Reformed minister had told her that there was such a thing as sin and that she was a sinner. She said, 'I was absolutely thrilled that somebody said there is something definitely wrong, there is such a thing as definite sin, there is a holy God and to go against his character is wrong and is sinful, and that I was in the wrong with God. I was thrilled because then I realised I could get in the right with God. For the first time I realised that there was something that worked.' This message can be as readily grasped within a relativistic culture as within a conservative one.

Good ministers would never wish to seem odd or vicious, but this valid concern can give us a tendency to blend in with the prevailing 'tolerant' relativism. We do not want to be seen as extreme, so we steer a middle road, so that we can be accepted. This is one of the most damaging things we can do to the souls of men and women (insofar as we let secularists define where lies the middle road). On the contrary, they need somebody to say, 'Enter through the narrow gate. For wide is the gate and broad is the road that leads to destruction, and many enter through it. But small is the gate and narrow the road that leads to life, and only a few find it' (Matt. 7:13-14).

One of the greatest contributions we can make is not just to say it, but actually to live in a way that demonstrates that some things are wrong and some things are right. How important this is for post-modern relativists! But to get anywhere with them, we will have to be real ourselves. Lack of personal integrity will ruin our proclamation of absolute truth. That is what happened with some of the American television evangelists. Undoubtedly they said some good things, but their lives totally denied what they were saying because they were not prepared to renounce certain things. The subsequent fall-out has been entirely negative. Any true Christian minister has got to renounce certain things in order to live the gospel and to speak in a credible way to a sceptical audience. It is not all that important to know terms like 'post-modernism' and 'post-structuralism', although undoubtedly some Christians are called to study them and to deal with them. What will totally destroy your ministry, however, is if you are mean to your wife and your children, if you do not pay your bills, if you are not moral in secret places, or if your true heart is set on the paltry honours and passing pleasures of this world. Until we have genuinely renounced in ourselves what needs to be renounced, we will have no lasting influence on the post-modernists whose relativism we may loudly decry.

Renouncing a worldly spirit

In the medieval church candidates for baptism had to declare, 'We renounce Satan and all his pomps.' The pompous show and pretence of the world is to be renounced for something vastly greater. Augustine said that God has made the human heart for himself and it is restless until it rests in him. Secularism, however, fails to see this and in its lust for quick pleasure loses touch with transcendent reality, as it seeks satisfaction in the material realm. Eclipsing heaven by concentrating on the material has sad ramifications. For example, when one does not have the genuine reality, then the appearance becomes over-important, so that politicians are elected on the basis of their looks rather than their beliefs. Even ministers can be tempted to cultivate their image for the sake of popularity. True, ministers are not supposed to look slovenly as if they did not respect their audience, but they are not to emphasise self or to be concerned about creating an impression of materialist elegance or personal cleverness. This sort of attitude takes over the more we lose sight of transcendent reality by failing to renounce self-centred, self-destructive goals.

So the apostle Paul says that one of the ways he has been able to concentrate on this gospel and see the glory of God come down, is that he has renounced certain things. He has to lay aside certain sins and temptations in order to allow the living gospel to reach the conscience. Although Scripture teaches that those who are unsaved do not have spiritual insight, still they are not idiots and they can often detect insincerity. They might not be able to put their finger on it, but in due time they can tell if we are not submitted to the patterns and the disciplines of the Word of God. For all the technical correctness of our theology, we will not break through to their conscience if we have not renounced a worldly spirit.

I believe the apostle is thinking of this when he refers to 'not handling the word of God deceitfully'. We must not use the Word to convey our cleverness or particular hobby–horse, nor must we dilute it in order to avoid offending certain groups or individuals. We must not make it easy so that people will think of us as 'a nice minister'. We will do well to die to such silly approval and instead follow, at least in spirit (if not in length and detail!), the preaching of the Puritans, which was rich in direct and uncomfortable application to the conscience, and relevant to their times so that people could understand it quite clearly. They were not commending themselves but lifting up Christ. They had renounced selfish goals in favour of letting the life of the Lord Jesus shine through to their needy audience.

A spiritual conflict

In verse 5 we find this very thing: 'For we do not preach ourselves, but Jesus Christ as Lord, and ourselves as your servants for Jesus' sake.' It is not by looking at the minister and being convinced of his ability that a supernatural thing occurs, but it is by keeping our emphasis on the Lord Jesus Christ. So, as he is held forth in true and anointed preaching of the Word, Paul warns us that the evil one will be present trying to blind people to keep them away from an offer so wonderful and so sensible. To refuse the sweet, loving offers of the Father, Son and Holy Spirit, you must almost have a suicidal impulse. It has to be an outside activity that is stirring the dregs of your fallen nature to make you want to destroy yourself by turning your back on God and despising the blood of the covenant.

In Ephesians 6:12 we read, 'For our struggle is not against flesh and blood, but against the rulers, against the authorities, against the powers of this dark world and against the spiritual forces of evil in the heavenly realms.' There are invisible observers every time the gospel is preached; the powers of good and evil are somehow struggling over the souls of men and women, because there are eternal implications for those souls for whom the preacher must give account. Even when Satan seems to be having a field day and successfully blinding the eyes of so many people, we are to keep on preaching and witnessing, as did Paul the apostle. We are not to faint, but to keep on receiving mercy and to keep on using the weapon of prayer (Eph. 6:18) as we deal with supernatural powers. This inevitable spiritual battle is just as difficult, and the resort to divine resources is just as necessary, in a culture of traditional morality(such as the pre-1960 American South in which I was brought up) as it is in a more openly licentious, post-modernist culture (as in Britain and America today). No culture has ever exempted Christians from self-denying spiritual battle, nor will any culture ever be able to hinder their effectiveness, if they fight the Lord's battles in the Lord's way.

'Let there be light' (v. 6)

Thirdly, in verse 6, we are given *the reason why Paul is able to endure* and to concentrate on the essentials in this battle that is not against flesh and blood: 'For God, who said, "Let light shine out of darkness," made his light shine in our hearts to give us the light of the knowledge of the glory of God in the face of Christ.' He is able to stick to the gospel even when many people reject it, when there is Satanic oppression, when the culture is going in the opposite direction. He looks not at himself but at the Lord, and he continues being a servant of these people at Corinth because this Lord Jesus has shined into his heart.

The verse harks back to Genesis 1:3, 'And God said, "Let there be light," and there was light.' He is drawing an analogy from the old creation where everything was dark until the beauty of God's light came in and turned a chaos into a cosmos. He is saying that God shines his light also in the new creation, but this time it is not something separable from God as created light was; this is uncreated light coming in the flesh of Jesus, who is the light and the glory of God. He who called himself 'the light of the world' shined into Paul to show the glory of God in the face of Jesus. That is the answer for the darkness of every culture: modernist, post-modernist or traditionalist. Show them the light! That is the triumphant weapon in the battle for souls in every culture.

Thomas Halyburton, one of the great Scottish theologians, wrote many years ago of his conversion in terms of this light which God showed him:

> I cannot be very positive about the day or the hour. It was towards the end of January 1698. So far as I can remember, I was at secret prayer in very great extremity, not far from despair when the Lord seasonably stepped in and gave this merciful turn to affairs. When I said there was none to save, then His arm brought salvation. God, who commanded the light to shine out of darkness, shined into my

mind. The Lord said to me, 'Thou hast destroyed thyself, but in me is thy help.' He made all His goodness pass before me and proclaimed His name. He revealed Christ in His glory and I was made by this sight to say, 'Thou art fairer than the sons of men.' I saw, moreover with wonder and delight, how God by this means might be just, even in justifying the ungodly who believe in Jesus. It was not indeed, by one particular promise or testimony of scripture but by the concurring light of a great many seasonably set home. But it was not the Bible alone that conveyed the discovery, for most of these passages whereby I was relieved, I had formerly in my distress read and thought upon without finding any relief in them. There was light in his words and a burning shining light by them shone into my mind. Not merely some doctrinal knowledge but the light of the knowledge of the glory of God in the face of Jesus Christ. That light that I now had, shone from heaven. It came by the word of God. It opened heaven and it led me up to heaven. It was a true light, a pleasant and a sweet light, a distinct and clear light, a satisfying, quickening refreshing, healing light. A powerful light. It was composing. It composed and quieted my soul and put all of my questions, as it were, in their due position and gave me all the exercise of them. No true idea of light is conveyed by words, you have to see it. But when you see it you know.

The apostle Paul had seen the glory of God in the face of Jesus and he could not keep it to himself. He proclaimed the truth and lived the truth, enduring, concentrating and receiving mercy. He renounced all unworthy goals in order to live in this light and to spread it. The glory of God came down and began to change an entire world one by one by one. It is the same today. The same glory can come down and work the most miraculous changes in a small community, a larger one, or a whole culture. As Jesus is lifted up, he will draw his own to himself and transform them. No culture, no matter how sophisticated its pretensions, can hold back this light. For the knowledge of the glory of the Lord, one day, shall cover the earth as the waters cover the sea. The glory of the one true God overwhelmed proud Rome with all of its relativism long ago. That same glory will by and by overwhelm the equally proud Western world with its own form of modernist (or post-modernist!) relativism. Renouncing all else to live and preach this glorious Christ should be our only concern, as it was the only concern of the apostle Paul. As Samuel Rutherford would remind us, 'Duties are ours; events are the Lord's.'

7

Transcendent Light through Broken Jars

2 Cor 4:7-18

[7]But we have this treasure in jars of clay to show that this all-
surpassing power is from God and not from us. [8]We are hard pressed
on every side, but not crushed; perplexed, but not in despair; [9]perse-
cuted, but not abandoned; struck down, but not destroyed. [10]We al-
ways carry around in our body the death of Jesus, so that the life of
Jesus may also be revealed in our body. [11]For we who are alive are
always being given over to death for Jesus' sake, so that his life may
be revealed in our mortal body. [12]So then, death is at work in us, but
life is at work in you.

[13]It is written:"I believed; therefore I have spoken." With that same
spirit of faith we also believe and therefore speak, [14]because we know
that the one who raised the Lord Jesus from the dead will also raise
us with Jesus and present us with you in his presence. [15]All this is for
your benefit, so that the grace that is reaching more and more people
may cause thanksgiving to overflow to the glory of God.

> [16]*Therefore we do not lose heart. Though outwardly we are wasting away, yet inwardly we are being renewed day by day.* [17]*For our light and momentary troubles are achieving for us an eternal glory that far outweighs them all.* [18]*So we fix our eyes not on what is seen, but on what is unseen. For what is seen is temporary, but what is unseen is eternal.*

Many years ago when I was a student in Edinburgh, I was completely taken aback at a Christian Union meeting, when the Reverend William Still stopped in the middle of a sermon, and in a loud voice cried out: 'Christ is in you, and is shouting, "I want out!"' That is the message of 2 Corinthians 4:7-18.

In the Old Testament book of Judges chapter 7, we are told the story of Gideon and his three hundred men who overcame the thousands of Midianites. Sometimes we feel as if we only have a few hundred people, as we face the millions of unbelievers in a culture that is not particularly glad to hear what God has commissioned us to tell them. But being in a minority has never been a problem with God. The Puritan expositor Matthew Henry says that in 2 Corinthians 4:7, the apostle Paul may have had the story of Gideon in mind when he writes 'we have this treasure in jars of clay to show that this all-surpassing power is from God and not from us.'

In Judges 7 the Lord led Gideon to reduce to three hundred the number of men who would defend Israel against these predatory Midianites. Then God gave Gideon a remarkable plan to overcome a massively larger enemy. Evidently the Midianites were down in a valley and it was late at night, totally dark. And so Gideon organised these three hundred men to stand on the tops of the hills that ring that valley, holding torches and trumpets. The light of these torches was inside a clay jar where it could get air and keep burning, yet remain hidden. At the given moment while the Midianites were sound asleep, Gideon's men broke those clay jars, put the trumpets to their lips and began to blare out the music, striking terror into the heart of the Midianites. For when the jars were broken the light was shining out, and victory was brought to the outnumbered people of God because the enemy panicked and fled. Matthew Henry suggests that this is what God is doing in a fruitful Christian ministry. There has to be a brokenness in the Christian's life, so that the resurrection light of the Lord Jesus may be able to shine out of us to illumine others and cause them to see through the darkness the bright face of the Lord Jesus Christ.

Treasure in clay jars (v. 7)

There are three strange contrasts in this text, from verses 7-18. Whenever there is a fruitful Christian ministry that is doing the work of God by winning the lost, and rolling back the darkness by spreading abroad the beauty of the Lord's love, there is a set of three unexpected things that go together as strange partners, like the wolf and the lamb in Isaiah 11:6. The first contrast in an effective Christian ministry, we are told in verse 7, is *heavenly treasure unexpectedly found in clay jars.* Verse 6 tells us what the treasure is. It is the light of God shining to give us the knowledge of the glory of God in realising who Jesus Christ is. Not only is he the One through whom all things were created, but he was incarnate in this world as God in the flesh. He lived a perfectly holy life, then stood in our place and died for the sins of all God's people. He took our humanity down into the place of death, then God the Father accepted his offering as more than sufficient to pay for all of our sins and raised his body to life again. This same Lord Jesus Christ, the crucified and risen and exalted One, sends down his Holy Spirit to shine forth the glory of his resurrection life into the forgiven ones, who will be in fellowship with him forever. That is the heavenly treasure that he has put in a clay jar: the very life of the triune God – the blissful fellowship of love between Father, Son and Holy Spirit – now flowing down to us.

In order to exercise faith in the Lord Jesus, the Holy Spirit works to open our eyes so that we see the light of who Jesus Christ is.

Heavenly treasure is being deposited in the strangest place: plain old fallen human nature in bodies that will eventually succumb to death and return to dust. Through the Fall of Adam our bodies have been marked by sin, disease and corruption, and our personalities have been twisted so that we do not make proper use of the marvellous powers God gave us when he made us in his image. It is in these bodies and personalities that he puts this most wonderful treasure. If that does not surprise us, we have not understood two things: first, how serious is the Fall, and secondly, how glorious, noble, holy and wonderful is the light of Christ's gospel.

The same resurrection light that was shining in the tomb when Jesus' body came out alive, was shining when he was received into the heavenly places and took his seat on the rainbow-circled throne beside God the Father almighty above the crystal sea. It is a wonderful matter to think that the very light that shines and radiates and sparkles in the heavenly places comes down into our earthly bodies and souls, never to depart. The same apostle who wrote 2 Corinthians refers in Colossians 1:27 to 'Christ in you, the hope of glory.' The first strange contrast: heavenly treasure that God is depositing in clay jars.

From death comes life (vv. 8ff.)

The second contrast that is found in a fruitful Christian life, and particularly an abounding Christian ministry, is that *when we die, life springs forth*. True children of God bear in themselves at the same time both a dying and a living. When we read the details of the second missionary journey of the apostle Paul in Acts 18, we can appreciate what it cost him to help establish a ministry in Corinth. He indicates what he means in verses 8-10: 'We are hard pressed on every side, but not crushed; perplexed, but not in despair; persecuted, but not abandoned; struck down, but not destroyed. We always carry around in our body the death of Jesus...' Nobody in their right mind enjoys that experience of being broken. As Jesus says in John 15:2, 'every branch that does bear fruit he prunes so that it will be even more fruitful.' Pruning is drastic, painful cutting, like a kind of death.

In Acts 16:7 the apostle was forbidden by the Holy Spirit to preach in Asia Minor, although he had been looking forward to visiting that area. But then he was guided by the Holy Spirit to the coast where he had a vision of a Macedonian telling him to come over and preach in the upper part of Greece. For a while the apostle did not know what he would do next. Some of the most fruitful men of God have had to wait a long time before a pulpit was opened to them. Some of the most fruitful congregations in different parts of the world take such a long time to find the right minister that they almost look foolish. It was like that with Paul. Sometimes we have to be willing not to know God's future plans for our lives, but just simply follow him, whatever the situation.

When dying becomes a door

So Paul followed the Lord's guidance to go to Greece, where he delivered a demon-possessed girl at Philippi, thus provoking a riot. As a result Paul was beaten and thrown into prison, yet out of the sufferings of his wounded, bleeding body the light of Christ was shining through to the Philippian jailer, who asked Paul and Silas, 'Sirs, what must I do to be saved?' Modern thinking would say that you must be impressive if you want to influence even a lower official of the Roman Empire like that jailer. You would need to show off how able and strong you are, and the connections you have with this, that and the other important person. Yet God has chosen the weak and the foolish things of this world to shame the strong, as Paul says in 1 Corinthians 1:27. God asks us to take what little we have and yield it up to him so that he can use it to do mighty, miraculous things through our weakness and our brokenness. God says 'Give it to me, trust me in the dark place. I can do far more with your weakness than with all the impressiveness and pomp of a worldly approach.' Paul's 'dying' became a door for the risen Lord Jesus to get through.

As we yield ourselves to have our selfishness broken, to have ourselves cancelled out so that the needs of others are put first, we experience something of the cross. As we bear about in the body the dying of the Lord Jesus, so we have the life of God flowing through us. As the jar was broken in the time of Gideon, out shines the light of glorious salvation and life in Christ.

A great Bible scholar of the nineteenth century, James Denney, said in his commentary on 2 Corinthians, 'Suffering for the Christian is not an accident. It is a divine appointment and a divine opportunity. To wear life out in the service of Jesus is to open it to the entrance of Jesus' life. It is to receive in all its alleviations, all its renewals and all its deliverances a witness to His resurrection. Perhaps it is only by accepting this service with the daily dying it demands that that witness can be given to us and the life of Jesus on His throne may become inapprehensible and unreal in proportion as we decline to bear about in our bodies His dying.' James Philip wrote a helpful article on preaching a number of years ago; here are two sentences that go right to the point of this text: 'Our lives are meant to reflect the death of Christ in such a way that men are somehow reminded of Calvary. We are to be signposts to Calvary and our lives must say to men, "Behold the Lamb of God that taketh away the sin of the world."'

C S Lewis, in his illuminating book *The Four Loves*, writes of how our hearts must be kept locked up in a casket of selfishness in order to avoid being broken. He says, 'The alternative to tragedy, or at least the risk of tragedy, is damnation. The only place outside of heaven where you can be safe from the dangers and perturbations of love is hell. We shall draw nearer to God, not by trying to avoid the sufferings inherent in love, but by accepting them, offering them back to Him, throwing away all defensive armour. If our hearts need to be broken, and if He chooses this way as the way in which they should break, so be it.' The price for the light to shine out of the clay pot is the breaking of the jar. In other words our Christian life, ministry, influence, resources, thinking, motivations, relationships and all that we are has to be continually yielded to God to be bent, broken, remade, refocused, renewed any way he wants to do it. There will always be a cost in having this light shining out of us, but God may cause this to happen in a different way for each of us.

Trouble yet glory (vv. 16ff.)

The third strange contrast, particularly in verses 16-18, that we find in a fruitful Christian ministry is *temporary trouble and eternal glory*. It is not our business to wring our hands over how awful it is today. Although we have to be realistic and admit the difficulties, we must not let them get the better of us. We yield ourselves to God in the knowledge that he will win, no matter how terrible the times. The Christian knows that temporary trouble always has along with it eternal glory that the world cannot see. In a sense even during our earthly pilgrimage, the trouble is sweetened and outweighed by the glory. This is the reason Paul could bear these sufferings. Who would like to have been criticised and misunderstood as he was, shipwrecked several times, beaten with rods and thrown into jail, ultimately waiting for his execution? Yet God is filling him with his glory and using him to change the world, so he is able to bear whatever God calls him to bear. He is willing to be crushed as many times as God wants his poor jar to be broken. He can even rejoice and be a tower of strength to others, because he looks in the direction of the unseen. He is not concentrating on the temporary troubles, although he is not foolishly unaware of them, but he is focusing on the eternal glory.

One choice we must make

We do not have a choice as to whether or not we suffer: that is in the providence of God. So we cannot choose whether we will always be healthy or popular, whether our children or spouse will do exactly as we wish, or whether our career will be successful. But as sons and daughters of God we do have one choice to make when the difficulties come. We can concentrate on the troubles and think of them all the time; we may begin to faint or develop a hurt, bitter spirit as we wonder why we no longer experience our former joy and fruitfulness. Alternatively, we can choose to concentrate on the eternal glory, as did the apostle Paul, who went through more than most of us. Evidently when Paul and Silas were in that Philippian jail, they were not concentrating on the wounds that they had received, but on the eternal glory as they sang psalms of praise to the Lord.

Our culture has tended to emphasise the material as the only reality, yet many people find that there is a witness in their hearts that there is a spiritual realm. Christians know that temporal things are passing, because in a sense believers are already in the eternal realm. God's Word testifies accurately to the unseen, unchanging, eternal things; as we focus on these realities they begin to lift us up and transform us. We can abide in whatever God's providence shall ask us to go through, and not only abide but be fruitful, Christ-like personalities, as we look not at the temporary troubles but at the eternal glory.

The eternal weight of glory

The great Scottish reformer, John Knox, died in his late 50s but apparently looked like a man in his 80s because he had suffered so much. He had been a captive in the hold of French galley ships, and he had been exiled and hounded day and night. John Knox was the minister of Saint Giles in Edinburgh, and one of the elders of the Kirk Session called on him the very day before he died. This elder said that he visited expecting to see a man who had at least one foot in the grave, and physically this was true. But the brightness and freshness and beauty of the resurrection morning was upon Knox's face and in the tones of his voice. Knox took this elder's hand and said something like this: 'I have been wrestling this night in the heavenly places and I've been down deep and wrestled with God for the soul of Scotland, that the Reformed faith would triumph in this land. The Lord has shown me that the Reformed Church will be severely and sorely tested in Scotland, but that it will triumph over all. And so God has led me within the veil and I'm ready to go home and live.' As it says in verse 16 the outer nature was perishing, but the inner nature was truly being renewed. John Knox was not looking at the temporary troubles he had been through in the cause of Reformation, but he was looking to the eternal glory and was dying in great joy.

As the hymn says:

I've found a Friend, O such a Friend!
All power to Him is given,
To guard me on my upward course,
And bring me safe to heaven.
The eternal glories gleam afar,
To nerve my faint endeavour;
So now to watch! to work! to war!
And then – to rest for ever.

Through death, life springs forth, the world is changed and souls are saved. The broken jars reveal the glory of the Lord Jesus, and our triune God is glorified.

8

Life's Most Generous Exchange

8: 2 Cor 5:1-8

> *[1]Now we know that if the earthly tent we live in is destroyed, we have a building from God, an eternal house in heaven, not built by human hands. [2]Meanwhile we groan, longing to be clothed with our heavenly dwelling, [3]because when we are clothed, we will not be found naked. [4]For while we are in this tent, we groan and are burdened, because we do not wish to be unclothed but to be clothed with our heavenly dwelling, so that what is mortal may be swallowed up by life. [5]Now it is God who has made us for this very purpose and has given us the Spirit as a deposit, guaranteeing what is to come.*
>
> *[6]Therefore we are always confident and know that as long as we are at home in the body we are away from the Lord. [7]We live by faith, not by sight. [8]We are confident, I say, and would prefer to be away from the body and at home with the Lord.*

The grand Scottish minister, Thomas Boston, suggested in his work *Man's Fourfold State* that when we give someone a cup of cold water in Christ's name, our generous God will one day give us 'a river of pleasure' in exchange for it. This astonishing generosity of God is in view in 2 Corinthians 5:1-8.

Life on the other side

The first question arising out of this text is: 'Why it is that the apostle Paul should introduce life after death at this particular point in the epistle?' The fourth chapter is a very realistic chapter on the high cost of a faithful Christian ministry. We are troubled, perplexed, persecuted, cast down. If we are identified with the Lord Jesus Christ, he will call us from time to time – fairly regularly, no doubt – to experience aspects of the cross in the form of death to self. There will be pressures that come on us from a society that does not want to hear that there are moral absolutes, that humans are sinful, and that the grace of God in the Lord Jesus Christ is our one and only hope. All kinds of criticisms, misunderstandings and troubles can come on us for just effectively proclaiming God's truth – the thing that people most need to hear. Some will hate us for it to start with, although when we persist some will undoubtedly turn to love us, though some will not. So in any serious Christian ministry we will be so closely allied to the Lord Jesus Christ in spirit and in motive that it profoundly affects the choices we make. Sometimes we have to choose death to self, in order that others can be blessed and God can be honoured.

Yet that is not the whole story of the Christian ministry. God has made us as humans to long for life and joy and blessing, and it is not unworthy to be motivated by these things. But we are to focus on the resurrection life, so chapter 5 talks about the glory of life on the other side of dying. Dr John Zizioulas has written a very interesting book entitled *Being as Communion*. Although I could not subscribe to all that he says, I learned much from his many helpful insights. One of the things that encouraged me and started me thinking was his statement that Christians are folk who have roots in two directions. We have roots in *the past* that help to define us, but the born-again child of God is also rooted in and defined by *the future*. It is as though we have roots up to heaven, up to the throne of God, up to the resurrection body, up to the final glorification that by grace the Lord will work in us. Ephesians 2:6 tells us that 'God raised us up with Christ and seated us with him in the heavenly realms...'

A glorious exchange

The second question arising from this text is: 'What happens to Christians after physical death?' Undoubtedly in chapter 4:10 the apostle is using death figuratively to represent our daily dyings to self when he says, 'We always carry around in our body the death of Jesus...' But in chapter 5 he is speaking literally of the physical death that awaits us all. It has been said that in the nineteenth century it was fine to talk about death but not sex, but in the twentieth century it is fine to talk about sex but not death. Some of the most 'liberated' people become quite offended if their own mortality is mentioned, and any discussion of physical death is held to be 'in poor taste'. Yet there is nothing more liberating, uplifting or empowering for an effective, fruitful, Christian ministry than to face our own mortality. Let us look it in the eye in the light of what the Lord Jesus has done and what our position is as believers. Nothing will strengthen us more to die to self when that is called for, or to put the Lord first, as is always called for. As we confront death personally, emotionally and theologically, there is a tremendous liberating power when we see our roots in the future, seated with Christ in the heavenly places.

After death? (v. 1f.)

Regarding specifically what happens to Christians upon their physical death, Paul uses the illustration of the tabernacle or 'earthly tent' in verse 1 of chapter 5. The tabernacle was that moveable tent in the wilderness, a temporary structure contrasted with the solid permanency of the stone temple. When the fiery, cloudy pillar, representing the glorious presence of God, began to move, the

Levites would fold up the tent and move on to the next spot on their pilgrimage to the promised land. So Paul compares our embodied human life to the temporary tent, not the enduring temple. Our physical existence is a wonderful gift of God and should in no sense be despised, but realistically it is like a fragile clay jar which can be broken at a stroke. The heavenly treasure is of course in these clay jars (4:7), but when in the providence of God the time comes for our physical death, then the jar is broken, as it were.

It reminds us of the description of physical death in Ecclesiastes 12:6, 'the silver cord is severed, or the golden bowl is broken...' All humankind is alike in the sense that to all shall come a breaking of the jar, a folding of the tent, a dissolving of the tabernacle, because death came upon all the human race through Adam's sin. But that is as far as the similarity goes between the believer and non-believer. After death everything is different for the unbeliever whose jar is broken compared to the believer. Death is never a final ending, much as secular humanists would like to think so, in order to avoid facing the idea of God's judgement. Perhaps their consciences are uneasy, which may explain why they are so offended by any mention of hell. If they were so sure it did not exist they could laugh it off.

This chapter does not contemplate to any degree what happens to unbelievers, but rather the wonderful exchange which takes place for the believer. The tattered tent is exchanged for something beautiful, valuable and permanent, given to us by our infinitely generous, loving and trustworthy God. Let us resist the lie that God is niggardly, mean and harsh. The evil one wants to misrepresent God even in the minds of those in the ministry. Sometimes we can feel that we serve a hard taskmaster, who hardly seems to answer our prayers. We can feel so hurt that we may be tempted to give up our vocation. Sometimes God entrusts us with suffering so that he can prune us to bear more fruit, but the process is painful. God does not approve of what wicked people may do to us; he will hold them to account and will vindicate those who belong to him. In the dark places when God allows trouble to afflict us, we can trust such a God who loved us so very much that he gave up to death the Son of his heart. We do not need to keep asking him, 'Why?' Instead we can ask 'What would you have me do, Lord? How will I carry on in a way that will bring you glory?'

From rags to riches

We are told in verse 1 that in physical death we exchange our worn-out tent for a beautiful house not made with hands, 'a building of God, eternal in the heavens'. I heard about an incident in the Hebrides that provides an illustration. An elderly woman on the Isle of Lewis had to move out of her old black house with its earthen floor and its thatched roof which was caving in. She was weeping and refusing to leave her home, but soon enough she was fine when she got into her new house with its damp-proof course and running water – it was far more comfortable. Death is like moving from a dilapidated hut to a beautiful palace; that's how generous God is going to be to us. If only we could by faith see through the veil. All we can see here is a loved one laid out in the coffin; we experience the end of the relationship we have known and the brokenness of human existence. But chapter 5 allows us to see through to another world – an open window with the curtains pulled slightly apart so that we can see a little of what is really there. Our secularist culture says that all things are relative and that all books are manifestations of the human spirit. It is not true. There is one book that comes from God, which functions like an X-ray allowing us to see beyond the surface of the human body.

'Clothed' (vv. 3ff.)

We notice in verse 3 that after death we shall not be found naked, but will be immediately clothed with this new eternal house. Exegetically it is unlikely that the text is referring to the final resurrection at the end of time; the passage is clearly speaking of the intermediate state before the last trumpet shall sound and all the saints are raised physically in glory. After death we are not denuded of personality or negated from who we most essentially are in Christ. All ideas of soul-sleep are contrary to the clear teaching of Holy Scripture. When it speaks of death as sleep, it refers to the idea of the body being still until the final resurrection. But the personality, the renewed, ransomed person that you and I are in Christ Jesus, carries on: 'then I shall know fully, even as I am fully known' (1 Cor. 13:12). Jesus said to the penitent thief on the cross, 'today you will be with me in paradise' (Luke 23:43). He is not saying, 'You are going to rise on the last day', although that is clearly taught in Scripture. But that is not the comfort Christ is giving him, true though it be. He is saying, 'This very day when you are pronounced dead, you are going with me into the place of refreshment and bliss and joy.'

When the Sadducees were questioning the reality of any personal existence beyond physical death, Jesus spoke about the God of Abraham, Isaac and Jacob: 'He is not the God of the dead, but of the living' (Mark 12:27). The point of this text is not that God is living, which the Sadducees granted, but that Abraham, Isaac and Jacob, whose bodies were by this time dust somewhere in Palestine, are alive in heaven. On the Mount of Transfiguration, Moses and Elijah were alive when they spoke to Jesus of the greater exodus which he should accomplish in Jerusalem. They encouraged him to go through it, as though their very resurrection and eternal well-being depended upon the Saviour going through Gethsemane and Calvary and coming out of that empty tomb.

One of the daily readings from Spurgeon's *Morning and Evening* asks the question, 'Why are our loved ones taken?' Sometimes a Christian family may be literally down on their very knees at the bedside praying for their loved one not to be taken. Sometimes their request is granted, but when God says, 'No' to those heartfelt prayers of a family, they feel quite broken. Why did God take someone whose life could have been so productive in Christian service? Then Spurgeon pictures the Lord Jesus Christ as the great High Priest in heaven, whose prayers are in a different direction. The Lord in his infinite wisdom and knowledge loves the person who is ill even better than the family does, and he is praying for that person to come now to share his glory.

What happens when I die?

We may ask what exactly is this 'eternal house in heaven, not built by human hands' in verse 1? The reality is that the physical body remains on earth and will not be reconstituted until the last trumpet heralds the general resurrection. John Calvin says in his commentary on 2 Corinthians, 'I prefer this building in heaven to mean that the blessed condition of the soul after death is the commencement or the beginning of this building and that the glory of the final resurrection is the consummation of it.' Calvin is saying that it is like the first stage or down payment, as if events to come cast their shadows before them. Maybe immediately after death we have a similarity in our state to what we shall ultimately be – a beauty, a sinlessness, a purity that in some way will correspond to the glorified resurrection body that we shall finally receive on the last day at the very end of time.

There are mysteries here that we cannot explain, but what we can say is that in this 'house... not built by human hands' we do see the Lord. 1 John 3:2 tells us that 'when he appears we shall be like him, for we shall see him as he is.' Is not the greatest distress of any true Christian minister that daily discovery of our unlikeness to the Lord Jesus? We may find that we are failing to practise the very thing we have preached. But there is coming a day when we shall see him and find that we are like him forever without sin. Perhaps it will be both the greatest shock and the greatest wonder of our lives. We will be able to praise and thank him while we wait for the final consummation of the resurrection of all who are in Christ. In the words of Augustine, 'In that day the rapture of the saved soul shall flow over into the glorified body.'

Groaning yet confident

The third question arising out of this text is: 'What is the Christian's attitude towards death?' Verse 6 declares, 'Therefore we are always confident', but verse 4 has the statement 'while we are in this tent, we groan and are burdened'. Realistically we would have to say that the true Christian's attitude towards their own mortality and that of others is a combination of both groaning and confidence. We live in both the seen and the unseen realms, and when these two worlds come together at the transition of death, there is an uncomfortable contradiction, like the turbulence produced when two great rivers merge. This is the groaning, as we sow in tears. Jesus wept at the tomb of Lazarus, even though he knew the future; therefore grief at bereavement cannot be a sign of a lack of faith, since Jesus had perfect faith. We groan because we sow in tears and we do not yet reap in joy. Evidently this is part of the broader groaning of the creation referred to in Romans 8:22 where the process is likened to painful childbirth. Something good will come out of it, but the pains of labour are upon the Christian. We are realistic about the sorrow and suffering of bereavement.

At the same time we have the confidence spoken of in verses 6-8: 'Therefore we are always confident and know that as long as we are at home in the body we are away from the Lord.' Not only confident but, in verse 8, 'would prefer to be away from the body and at home with the Lord'. It is good to be here, but there is somewhere that is even better when God's time comes for that. One of the early Methodist preachers was reproached by a member of the established church in these terms: 'The Methodists are not very distinguished people. They are not folk of particularly high or influential standing to say the least. And those are the elements who are following the likes of you.' The preacher looked at this man with a cordial smile and said to him, 'Yes, it may be so, but at very least the Methodists die well.' This is the confidence that sustains us: a solid foundation of faith that what our physical eyes cannot see really is there, and most of all there is a person there waiting to be gracious to us.

There was an American missionary, Mr E H Hamilton, who was in China during the 1930s and 40s. One of his colleagues, an American missionary named John Vinson, was accosted by armed Chinese bandits and forced at gunpoint to hand over his money. The bandits were astonished that this man was very calm and kindly, instead of showing anger or fear. One of the bandits said, 'I don't believe you understand. We have the power to kill you and we think we probably will kill you.' Mr Vinson answered immediately, 'Well, you can do that if you want to but it will take me immediately into the presence of the Lord. That's all you can do – I'll be with him.' The bandits did kill this missionary, but one of the bandits was so affected by what had happened that he later recounted the whole story, and his life was eventually transformed. When E H Hamilton heard the story, he wrote this poem entitled *Afraid? Of what?*:

Afraid? Of what?
To feel the spirit's glad release?
To pass from pain to perfect peace,
The strife and strain of life to cease?
Afraid – of that?

Afraid? Of what?
Afraid to see the Saviour's face,
To hear His welcome, and to trace
The glory gleam from wounds of grace?
Afraid – of that?

Afraid? Of what?
A flash – a crash – a pierced heart;

Darkness – light – Oh, Heaven's art!
A wound of His a counterpart!
Afraid – of that?

Afraid? Of what?
To enter into Heaven's rest,
And yet to serve the Master blest,
From service good to service best?
Afraid – of that?

Afraid? Of what?
To do by death what life could not:
Baptise with blood a stony plot,
Till souls shall blossom from the spot?
Afraid – of that?

Some of you may feel, that what is happening now in your lives or your ministry is, figuratively speaking, baptising with blood a very stony plot; if so, I want to exhort you to be faithful to Christ. His resurrection is stronger than all the powers of death; souls shall blossom from the spot and God will, in his good time, bring you into the glory and bring many souls with you. Isn't that enough to know? Isn't that enough to keep us faithful? Isn't that enough to make us ask, not 'Why me, Lord? Why is the other successful and I'm not?' but instead to be asking, 'What will you have me do, Lord?' May the sheer generosity of the exchange he has in store for us encourage us to yield everything afresh to him!

9

Resurrection Before Death

9: 2 Cor 5:9-21

[9]So we make it our goal to please him, whether we are at home in the body or away from it. [10]For we must all appear before the judgment seat of Christ, that each one may receive what is due him for the things done while in the body, whether good or bad. [11]Since, then, we know what it is to fear the Lord, we try to persuade men.What we are is plain to God, and I hope it is also plain to your conscience. [12]We are not trying to commend ourselves to you again, but are giving you an opportunity to take pride in us, so that you can answer those who take pride in what is seen rather than in what is in the heart. [13]If we are out of our mind, it is for the sake of God; if we are in our right mind, it is for you. [14]For Christ's love compels us, because we are convinced that one died for all, and therefore all died. [15]And he died for all, that those who live should no longer live for themselves but for him who died for them and was raised again.

[16]So from now on we regard no one from a worldly point of view. Though we once regarded Christ in this way, we do so no longer. [17]Therefore, if anyone is in Christ, he is a new creation; the old has

> *gone, the new has come!* [18]*All this is from God, who reconciled us to himself through Christ and gave us the ministry of reconciliation:* [19]*that God was reconciling the world to himself in Christ, not counting men's sins against them. And he has committed to us the message of reconciliation.* [20]*We are therefore Christ's ambassadors, as though God were making his appeal through us. We implore you on Christ's behalf: Be reconciled to God.* [21]*God made him who had no sin to be sin for us, so that in him we might become the righteousness of God.*

Christian art, music and preaching traditionally summarise Christ's life under the two themes of cross and empty tomb. The order of saving events is that he dies for our sins first and then rises again into victorious life. Thus for Christ it is death and then resurrection. But in a certain sense for the Christian the order is reversed. In the believer's experience of grace, Christ first raises us from our spiritual death into ever-living union with himself. Then he calls us willingly to accept many deaths for his sake in reaching a lost world. Romans 12:1 reflects this order of resurrection and then death, and then new resurrections for the believer: 'Therefore, I urge you, brothers, in view of God's mercy, to offer your bodies as living sacrifices, holy and pleasing to God – this is your spiritual act of worship.' This strange but miraculously fruitful order: resurrection, death, resurrection, is worked out in terms of victorious Christian ministry in 2 Corinthians 5:9-21.

The movement of the passage

First, let us consider the movement of the passage in its wider context. Verses 1-8 of the chapter are speaking of the benefit of leaving this world and going into the other world. Paul describes the blessings of the resurrection of Christ in raising the soul, saving the soul and upon physical death taking it into a place of bliss to wait for the final resurrection. Precisely after we are assured that we share in the resurrection victory of the Lord Jesus, verses 9-21 speak of the figurative deaths to self that God calls us to, then through those 'deaths' come resurrection experiences in and for others to the glory of God. In chapter 4 we had the high cost of the Christian ministry and the 'deaths' involved in that. In chapters 1–3 we had our union with Christ in the new covenant by the eternal design of the Father, through the Holy Spirit bringing us into the resurrection life of the Lord Jesus Christ. So the pattern is resurrection-death-resurrection-death-resurrection.

Resurrection-death-resurrection

When you become a Christian, it is as if God baptises you into this pattern of existence. Much of the time we experience life in a piecemeal fashion, and we are not aware of the overall plan. But when we look back over the influence of a Christian life, however, for example at a funeral, we can often discern a pattern of a cost to self, followed by influence on others bursting forth. In turn there will be more cost to self and more testings, out of which we can emerge into a place of blessing and influence. The very same pattern of ministry enabled a handful of fishermen who had been touched with the message, transformed by meeting this crucified, risen Redeemer, and indwelt by his Spirit to embark on the ministry of reconciliation. The very same pattern of dying to self and living to Christ, death working in them and life in others, is described in chapter 4:10. This pattern repeats itself over the years to those who will give themselves to Christ, and then to others for the sake of Christ. This pattern can transform any culture, no matter how anti-Christian it has become, and can overcome every opposition to truth, righteousness, goodness and beauty. C S Lewis once wisely wrote: 'We do not know more resurrections than we do in our Christian experience day by day, because of the deaths we refuse to die.'

In the sixth volume of the writings of the great Puritan theologian, John Owen, sanctification is seen as having two aspects: both 'mortification', or dying to self, and 'vivification', or living to the

Lord. Owen seems to be saying that the believer starts from a position of resurrection, as one who has been united to Christ and made alive in him. In the Father's love we have a source of security, life and joy; we breathe the atmosphere of heaven perhaps when we are least feeling it. It is as a risen one in the Lord Jesus Christ that God calls us to make all of our sacrifices in the Christian life, through which resurrection blessing is brought to others. Thus the movement of this passage in 2 Corinthians corresponds to this pattern of resurrection-death-resurrection.

The motives of Paul's ministry

Second, consider the motives of Paul's ministry, which are presented in verses 11-16. How could he have lived such an active and fruitful life, managing to write more of the New Testament than any other person? Two motives stand out as of prime importance: fear of Christ's judgement and knowledge of Christ's love. First, Paul fears Christ as judge. Does this conflict with the New Testament teaching that the blood of Christ delivers us from judgement? This passage is not referring to salvation, but to the assessment of our ministry. It is not a question of whether or not we will get into heaven. We can know that now in the assurance of the Holy Spirit on the basis of the Scriptures. Rather it is a question of how we have spent our lives in response to the grace of God. My whole life will be assessed by the One who knows how much he loved me; I must stand before him face to face, while beholding all that I did with my life and all that he gave me.

Christ as judge (v. 11)

Fear of Christ as judge was a proper motivating factor for the fruitfulness of Paul's ministry. Some people might object that such a motivation is unworthy, and so it would be if it were not true. But what if a building were on fire and you were shouting, 'Fire! Fire! Get out!' and throwing bricks through the window or bashing the door in to get the people out? No one would criticise you for responding to the reality of the situation. The reality of the divine assessment is a valid and an important motivation for every Christian. By way of illustration, there was an old-established Christian family business supplying all sorts of farm equipment in a small North Carolina town. One night it was totally burned to the ground, and because the owners were under-insured it was never rebuilt. Imagine how that family felt when they saw the work of three or four generations of the family going up in smoke and reduced to dust. Christians will feel far worse if we hold back in a miserly spirit from offering our best to the Lord Jesus, even though it might have been painful. In 1 Corinthians 3:13 Paul says that our work will be tested as if through fire; the end product will either be dross or precious gold. It does not matter how much influence we may think we have; what counts is that we are willing to give ourselves totally to the Lord, so that he can use us in the midst of this culture in whatever way he chooses. That is the basis on which we shall be assessed.

Christ's love (v. 14f.)

The second motivation of Paul's ministry is Christ's redemptive love to his people. This is the most powerful motivator, for Paul speaks of it *compelling* him. We are called to be faithful to that pattern of truth delivered to the saints once for all; we offer ourselves to God to show forth to others the dying and resurrection of Christ. Even when God's pruning hurts us, the thing that will make us go back to the pruning shears when called for, is that the love of Christ forces us. The word 'compels' in 5:14 (translated as 'constrains' in the Authorised Version) is the same verb which is used of the crowds pressing in on Jesus, so that he once had to get into a boat. It is as if the love of the Lord grips us in a vice, so that we can do nothing else but say 'Lord, here I am. Use me as you will.' The apostle Paul says, 'That's why I'm going to all these places, undergoing the ship-wrecks, the stonings, the beatings, the fastings, the defeats as well as the victories, because the love of the Lord Jesus is so real that it presses me in.'

The American evangelist Dwight L Moody, who was used of the Lord in Scotland in the 1880s, used to say that if love does not motivate us, then all of our work counts for nothing. Count Von Zinzendorf was an extremely wealthy nobleman in Germany, who one day saw in a museum a marvellous painting of Christ crucified. There was an inscription in Latin on the bottom of that painting, which translated into English as, 'I have done all for Thee. What hast thou done for me?' The love of Jesus broke through to this great nobleman; he thought that if Jesus Christ the Son of God would come and do that much for one who did not deserve it, then he would give him everything he had. He was constrained by the love of Christ to start the Moravian mission, out of which came a hundred years of prayer meetings day and night for missions, and the foundation of the modern missionary movement.

We need nothing more in God's church today in every country than a baptism of the love of the Lord Jesus afresh, constraining us in a God-ward direction. Ultimately this constraint is the same love that the Father has to the Son through the Holy Spirit, a love which Augustine called 'the bond of charity'. Romans 5:5 says, 'God has poured out his love into our hearts by the Holy Spirit, whom he has given us.' It is as if the triune God takes the lavish, abundant love that is in his own heart, the greatest treasure of heaven, and puts it in us. It is this kind of love that has motivated the Christian church for the past two thousand years. Far from being beaten down, and having its lamp put out, the church keeps rising up again. This is Paul's double motivation: he is constrained by the love of Christ, and he desires never to disappoint the Lord Jesus when he looks back on his life.

The message of Paul's ministry

Third, there is the message of Paul's ministry. It is essentially that there is one death in all the world that is supremely good news. The gospel is based on what would seem to worldly thinking the worst possible news – a death! But the apostle says that this particular death – what motivated it, what follows it and who was involved – is the power or the engine that turns and changes everything that ever was or ever shall be. First, Paul deals in the early part of chapter 5 with the reality of sin that brought death. Many people will say, 'Why would sin need to be punished if God is a God of love? Why does the evangelical wing of the Christian church have to keep talking about sin, punishment, blood and hell? We thought God was a God of love. Why is he demanding vengeance and why has that got to be the centre of the message? Can't we have something more desirable and pleasant than such a message?' When the modern church started to adapt itself to such demands, we abandoned the message, lost the power and saw our culture turn secular.

Why must God punish sin? Why is the statement in verse 21, 'God made him who had no sin to be sin for us, so that in him we might become the righteousness of God', the centre of Paul's message? Why is this idea of Jesus taking the place of the sinner the event that transforms everything else, that makes all wrongs right, that changes death into glorified life, condemnation into justification? The reason is that the seriousness of the sin is determined by the greatness of the person against whom you sin. Anselm said, 'Sin is determined by the nature of the person against whom you commit that sin.' God is an infinite person. Sin against a holy God is infinite sin, thus making the individual infinitely guilty. God's righteous justice must be satisfied, otherwise absolute justice would cease to exist. For God not to strike out against sin would be to leave a cancer that would eat up the whole universe, remove the Creator from his throne and destroy everything. God would have to deny his character not to deal with sin in proper moral measure.

The 'wondrous exchange'

The greatest problem of every man and woman, little though they realise it, is that we are finite, limited beings guilty of infinite sin against an infinite, holy, wonderful God. How can we deal with this? See, as Anselm said, the wisdom and love of our God. What his holiness requires his love provides, in that he sends his eternal Son to become a man. Thus he is an infinite person in human nature. He can represent God from the side of his infinity. He can represent you and me from the side of his humanity. He is the God-man, the mediator between God and man. Paul tells us that this is the greatest thing that ever happened – far greater than the creation of the universe out of nothing in the space of six days. The Creator enters the creation, becoming a creature without ceasing to be the Creator; somehow in those moments on the cross he becomes totally identified with all the sins of all those who will ever be saved through him.

John Calvin called what happened on the cross a 'wondrous exchange'. God the Father takes all of my sin, shame and guilt with the consequential death and hell, and places it on the holy, innocent and righteous head of God the Son. In exchange, the Father takes all of the Son's holiness, obedience, love and purity, and places it on my poor, sinful head, so that I am made fit for heaven. Any man or woman having their spiritual blindness removed by the Holy Spirit, so that they look upon this Lord Jesus with faith, becomes a new creation. Just as the old creation was made out of nothing, so a miracle of God occurs when a sinner looks to Jesus Christ for salvation:

> Upon a life I did not live,
> Upon a death I did not die,
> Another's life, another's death,
> I stake my whole eternity.

Paul tells us that it is this message that transforms everything.

The method of Paul's ministry

Finally, consider the method of Paul's ministry. In verse 20 Paul speaks of himself as an ambassador, who represents a government that has given him a message to declare, which he is not at liberty to change. Paul is deeply moved by this message; he is constrained by the perilous state of people's souls, the seriousness of their need and the greatness of the love of the Lord Jesus. Robert Trail, a great Scottish theologian of a previous generation, writing on the subject of how ministers may best win souls, said, 'If you would win souls, purchase and maintain the people's love.'

'Try tears'

General Booth of the Salvation Army once advised a very discouraged officer who was tempted to give up, 'Try tears.' The following incident shows the powerful effect this can have. A girl from a small country chapel married a high-ranking, well-educated army officer who was perhaps a bit proud of his accomplishments. When he visited his wife's relatives, a farm woman from the chapel tried to talk to this man about his soul. Although he tried to be polite, his dismissive laughter was barely concealed. When this farm wife saw his indifference and thought of the eternity he must face without the Lord Jesus, she began to weep. The officer was at the church that night, weeping himself because he realised he needed to come to Christ for salvation. He saw that all his military honours would get him nowhere but hell, and that life was not worth living without the Lord Jesus Christ. He later testified that it had been the tears of this farm wife with far less formal education than he had, but with wisdom from another world, that broke through to him.

Jesus commends that to us when he wept over the state of Jerusalem in Luke 19:41. Psalm 126:6 says: 'He who goes out weeping, carrying seed to sow, will return with songs of joy, carrying sheaves with him.' Our Lord deserves that every one of us shall say, 'Lord, here I am, yielding whatever I have to you to be used in accordance with your invisible pattern of truth – death to self, rising with you, and then life bursting forth in others.' All the tears shall be repaid with the most exquisite bearing-in of the harvest.

Risen ones (which is what believers already are in their renewed spirits) are called to accept many tears and deaths to self in order that others may thereby come to new life and eternal gladness. This supernatural process guarantees that all of them will – on the other side of the nails and pruning shears – rejoice together in fuller experiences of Christ's resurrection power, by which alone dying cultures can be transformed.

10

Investment Advice

10: 2 Corinthians 8

[1]And now, brothers, we want you to know about the grace that God has given the Macedonian churches. [2]Out of the most severe trial, their overflowing joy and their extreme poverty welled up in rich generosity. [3]For I testify that they gave as much as they were able, and even beyond their ability. Entirely on their own, [4]they urgently pleaded with us for the privilege of sharing in this service to the saints. [5]And they did not do as we expected, but they gave themselves first to the Lord and then to us in keeping with God's will. [6]So we urged Titus, since he had earlier made a beginning, to bring also to completion this act of grace on your part. [7]But just as you excel in everything—in faith, in speech, in knowledge, in complete earnestness and in your love for us -see that you also excel in this grace of giving.

[8]I am not commanding you, but I want to test the sincerity of your love by comparing it with the earnestness of others. [9]For you know the grace of our Lord Jesus Christ, that though he was rich, yet for your sakes he became poor, so that you through his poverty might become rich.

[10]And here is my advice about what is best for you in this matter: Last year you were the first not only to give but also to have the desire to do so. [11]Now finish the work, so that your eager willingness to do it may be matched by your completion of it, according to your means. [12]For if the willingness is there, the gift is acceptable according to what one has, not according to what he does not have. [13]Our desire is not that others might be relieved while you are hard pressed, but that there might be equality. [14]At the present time your plenty will supply what they need, so that in turn their plenty will supply what you need. Then there will be equality, [15]as it is written: "He who gathered much did not have too much, and he who gathered little did not have too little."

[16]I thank God, who put into the heart of Titus the same concern I have for you. [17]For Titus not only welcomed our appeal, but he is coming to you with much enthusiasm and on his own initiative. [18]And we are sending along with him the brother who is praised by all the churches for his service to the gospel. [19]What is more, he was chosen by the churches to accompany us as we carry the offering, which we administer in order to honor the Lord himself and to show our eagerness to help. [20]We want to avoid any criticism of the way we administer this liberal gift. [21]For we are taking pains to do what is right, not only in the eyes of the Lord but also in the eyes of men. [22]In addition, we are sending with them our brother who has often proved to us in many ways that he is zealous, and now even more so because of his great confidence in you. [23]As for Titus, he is my partner and fellow worker among you; as for our brothers, they are representatives of the churches and an honor to Christ. [24]Therefore show these men the proof of your love and the reason for our pride in you, so that the churches can see it.

[1]There is no need for me to write to you about this service to the saints. [2]For I know your eagerness to help, and I have been boasting about it to the Macedonians, telling them that since last year you in Achaia were ready to give; and your enthusiasm has stirred most of

them to action. [3]But I am sending the brothers in order that our boasting about you in this matter should not prove hollow, but that you may be ready, as I said you would be. [4]For if any Macedonians come with me and find you unprepared, we—not to say anything about you—would be ashamed of having been so confident. [5]So I thought it necessary to urge the brothers to visit you in advance and finish the arrangements for the generous gift you had promised. Then it will be ready as a generous gift, not as one grudgingly given.

[6]Remember this: Whoever sows sparingly will also reap sparingly, and whoever sows generously will also reap generously. [7]Each man should give what he has decided in his heart to give, not reluctantly or under compulsion, for God loves a cheerful giver. [8]And God is able to make all grace abound to you, so that in all things at all times, having all that you need, you will abound in every good work. [9]As it is written:

> *"He has scattered abroad his gifts to the poor;*
> *his righteousness endures forever."*[1]

[0]Now he who supplies seed to the sower and bread for food will also supply and increase your store of seed and will enlarge the harvest of your righteousness. [11]You will be made rich in every way so that you can be generous on every occasion, and through us your generosity will result in thanksgiving to God.

[12]This service that you perform is not only supplying the needs of God's people but is also overflowing in many expressions of thanks to God. [13]Because of the service by which you have proved yourselves, men will praise God for the obedience that accompanies your confession of the gospel of Christ, and for your generosity in sharing with them and with everyone else. [14]And in their prayers for you their hearts will go out to you, because of the surpassing grace God has given you. [15]Thanks be to God for his indescribable gift!

How much are people willing to pay for advice on how to invest their money successfully? I was surprised when I found out just how much some wealthy people would pay for such advice, when I was lecturing in some of the north-western states of the USA many years ago. A man who was very successful in giving investment advice on the commodities markets had an interest in Christianity, and invited me to his large office building in order to discuss some spiritual issues which were on his mind. During our discussion, he answered the telephone three or four times. He apologised for doing so, but said he had to talk to these people at once, because he had a number of customers who paid him something like $250 per month for the privilege of ringing him four or five times a week to talk about the direction the commodities market was taking. (My first – unspoken – thought was: nobody pays me anything for discussing life and death spiritual issues!) But it did teach me how highly motivated some people are to get investment advice, when they think it is worthwhile.

There is a sense in which we could call this fairly extended Scripture passage 'Investment Advice'. Undoubtedly there are principles which obtain in the financial and the natural world, just as there are principles which obtain in the spiritual realm of wise investment of life and resources. As I have just observed, people will pay considerable amounts of money to get good financial advice; how much more important to heed advice in the spiritual realm, which counts for eternity. Accepting such advice leads to joyful fruitfulness on earth and bliss in heaven, but rejecting it brings the certainty of the most appalling and inescapable bankruptcy.

Those who have invested their lives in the ministry sometimes lose sight of its long-term significance because of the pressures of the daily round of duties: the phone calls, hospital visits, funerals, weddings, parish visits, committee meetings, sermon preparation, and on top of all this, criticism to be endured. We can be so busy and tired that we begin to lose sight of the overall picture, the great pattern and purpose of our ministry. The love of Jesus constrained us to give up all else and to invest ourselves totally into this ministry, yet we may grow discouraged and frustrated and lose sight of the great overarching goal for which we were called. There is a time to step back and to think of the value, the beauty and the joy of having chosen this investment of our life and our resources.

The context in this passage is that the Corinthians needed encouragement to give generously for the financial needs of the Jewish saints in Jerusalem, who were then in economic downturn and difficult straits due to various forms of persecution. In chapters 8, 9 and part of 10, the apostle Paul encourages the Corinthians to be generous for three reasons. First, he cites the example of the Macedonians; secondly, the example of the Lord Jesus Christ; thirdly, he outlines the laws of blessing or investment principles that operate slowly but surely in God's world in both spiritual and physical realms as God deems appropriate.

An example of generosity (8:1ff.)

First, the apostle encourages the Corinthians to emulate the generosity of the Macedonian Christians who were extremely poor, by contrast with the wealthy economy of Corinth. The epistle to the Philippians, perhaps the most joyful letter in all of the New Testament, is written to these Macedonians. John Calvin brings out in his commentary that Macedonia was an economically deprived area because there had been a rebellion there against Rome, leading to economic persecution. As a result the Macedonians were some of the poorest people in the Roman Empire, yet the Christians there were some of the world's happiest people. Paul was very proud of them, and deeply touched by the sacrificial giving that they practised towards him. In chapter 8:2 he says, 'Out of the most severe trial, their overflowing joy and their extreme poverty welled up in rich generosity.'

A forgotten key to spiritual growth

The fact that the Macedonian Christians were both extremely poor and extremely joyful, practising self-sacrificial generosity, raises serious questions about our materialistic view of life. The whole of the advertising industry is built on persuading us to feel needs; it says to us, 'If you could get this you would be happier, so buy this and even indeed go into debt for it.' The statistics of debt now are alarming, and it has become one of the major causes of marriage difficulties. One of the reasons for so much appalling debt is that people actually believe that if they just have some more things their hearts might begin to be satisfied. In Luke 16:11 Jesus refers to 'unrighteous mammon' (the AV translation here is preferable to the NIV's weaker 'worldly wealth') as an idol which beckons to us, inviting us to establish a relationship with it. Mammon says, 'if you trust me, if you give your heart to me, I'll give you security and happiness and fulfilment'. But although in one sense it is neutral, yet when it enters into a relationship with us it deceives us because it never delivers what it promises. Jesus says that if we have been unfaithful in unrighteous mammon, who will trust us with the true riches?

This passage, coming as it does after the parable of the unjust manager, teaches us that there is no spiritual growth, no true riches, no blessing of God unless we handle what he has entrusted to us faithfully and rightly. One of the reasons for the spiritual decline of churches today is that the shadow of the world's hand has come over us. We have imperceptibly become as materialistic as those who are not believers, and our lifestyles are no different from unbelievers who are on the same salary.

By contrast, how is it that the Macedonians could have such deep poverty and such joyful generosity? Verse 1 makes it clear that it was the grace of God bestowed upon them. The sovereign God gave Paul that dream of the Macedonian call so that the gospel might be preached to them. The first convert in Europe was a Philippian woman named Lydia, whose heart was opened by God to receive the message of salvation. Thus we see the divine initiative, but also the human response in verse 5: 'they gave themselves first to the Lord and then to us in keeping with God's will.' As their hearts were opened, they offered themselves personally to the Lord Jesus, and therefore to his service and to his people. The key to their response is the word 'generosity' ('liberality' in the AV) in verse 2, meaning a simplicity of spirit that reversed the normal values of that pagan culture. In the book of Acts one of the pagan criticisms of Paul and his co-workers was that these people 'have turned the world upside down.' (Acts 17:6, AV)

A sweet simplicity of spirit

Although there is very much a place for intellectual answers to the problems of the day, still the key to transforming our secular, cynical, materialistic society is the sweet, generous simplicity of spirit seen in the lives of God's people. This is one of the church's most powerful weapons, together with prayer and the Word of God. Secularism promotes egocentric selfishness by saying, 'You'd better enjoy what you can while you can. You'll get old, it'll soon be gone, you'd better do it today, or it will be too late. Get whatever you can out of this. Everybody else is selfish, so you have every right to be selfish.' This is a normal way of thought for the natural man, which is one of the reasons that so many marriages are breaking up. But when people see somebody who is motivated by the atmosphere of a different world, they realise that this is something genuine. We may preach well on Sunday, but how we live in the community cannot be faked. If people see someone who is not motivated by selfish opportunism, but puts others first, they realise that something else is making that person kind and generous, and they begin to ask questions.

Christian compassion

Studies of the social and cultural impact of the early Christian church have shown that it was not only effective in preaching the gospel, but also in its care for the needs of others. For example, during the first three centuries of the Christian era in Rome, unwanted babies were abandoned under the bridges of the river Tiber, where they would be killed by wild dogs. But the Christians organised squads round these bridges and took the babies to their homes and cared for them as part of their family. It is not generally realised that this is a reason why so many people became Christians. At one stage the Roman Senate passed legislation making it illegal for Christians to gather up the babies, because the pagans were beginning to disbelieve the false rumours that were circulated about the Christians, such as the alleged practice of cannibalism. Many of Rome's elderly people were also abandoned to die out in the streets, and again the Christians would take them into their homes. Many of them recovered and became Christians too.

We are told in the Old Testament that God will not give his glory to another; it was death to come into the Holy of Holies, for the glory of God could kill those who were impure. Yet 8:23 makes the remarkable statement that these Macedonians are 'an honour to Christ', translated in the AV as 'the glory of Christ'. The greatest thing our secular society needs to see is the glory of Christ manifested in flesh and blood, the practical beauty of the love, purity and selflessness of the Lord Jesus in human personality. It is like planting a bomb of beauty and love and transformation amongst the secularists; they cannot behold the glory of Christ in a human life and stay the same when the Holy Spirit is working.

The example of Christ (8:9ff.)

Secondly, they are encouraged to be generous by the supreme example of Christ himself. In verse 9 of chapter 8 we read, 'For you know the grace of our Lord Jesus Christ, that though he was rich, yet for your sakes he became poor...' He laid aside the heavenly glory of his trinitarian life in order to become man. Without ceasing to be God he humiliated himself to the depths of the cross and death and hell, going deeper than we could ever go. For this reason 'God exalted him to the highest place and gave him the name that is above every other name...' (Phil. 2:5-11). Christ takes our humanity with him in his death and resurrection life; he impoverished himself to make countless people eternally rich. The Lord Jesus gave all and instead of losing, he gained the church and the renewed universe.

Keep on giving

The principle must always be the same: in the ministry we do not lose by giving. The devil says to us, particularly when we are tired and feel unappreciated, 'Hold back, protect your turf more, don't be giving this much, they don't appreciate it, they are not worth it, it's not any good, you've got to look after yourself, don't let yourself be bothered like this, they're not bothered, don't sacrifice so much, because if you give you lose.' The truth is quite the opposite: you give and others gain, because 'death is at work in us, but life is at work in you' (2 Cor. 4:12). They gain because the glory of the Lord is spreading; you gave and you are uplifted, but you have to walk by faith and not by sight. Do not walk by sight or feeling in the ministry because if you do you will hold back. In this matter we must walk by faith and keep on giving more because of the Lord Jesus Christ. When we look at his utter humiliation it seemed that the devil had conquered him, yet out of the worst thing that the devil could ever do comes the salvation of God's church and renewal of all creation.

The divine law (8:11-15 and chapter 9)

Thirdly, in chapter 9 we are exhorted to become generous by reason of God's laws of blessing. Chapter 8 verses 11-15 teach that we are to give a regular portion of what we have, according to the Old Testament at least a tithe (a tenth). Christ said that he had come not to abolish the law but to fulfil it, so surely grace should make us not less generous than the Old Testament, but more so. I suggest that the starting point should be 10 percent of our income, and then more as God leads us. God does not ask you to give on the basis on what you may inherit or earn later, but on the basis of what you have right now. If we do not tithe what we have now, then that may keep us from being blessed with more. 'He that is faithful with a little shall be faithful in much', and if God sees that he cannot trust us to give back a regular portion of what we have now, how can he trust us with more?

The oldest insurance company in the USA is the Presbyterian Ministers' Life Insurance, dating back to the 1750s. Its motto is taken from the AV translation of 2 Corinthians 9:6, 'He which soweth sparingly shall reap also sparingly and he which soweth bountifully shall reap also bountifully.' It is very clearly being taught that the more we give out of love for Christ, the greater the blessing the Lord is in a position to entrust us with. It is not only the law of the harvest that we reap what we sow, it is also the law of increase: give more and then God can entrust you in various ways with more.

There are many examples of this principle at work. A man who was superintendent of the state school system attended church with his Christian wife, although he himself was not converted. After he heard a sermon about tithing he decided, in consultation with his wife, to give God 10 percent. Within a few weeks he was gloriously saved. Jesus Christ's blood and righteousness paid for his salvation; it was not earned by his tithing. But there was something about letting go of what was very precious to this man, which opened the door for him to receive God's salvation.

Another man had a very difficult relationship with his father, which made it hard for him to feel the love of God or have assurance of salvation. After he decided to start tithing, he had a wonderful experience of the love of God warming his heart and giving him full assurance. Again his tithing did not pay for his assurance; Christ's death and resurrection purchased his assurance, but the act of committing himself in sacrifice let loose the blessing.

Another man who was a dedicated preacher in a poor area of North Carolina used to give supplies to poor people, many of whom were converted in a time of revival. At one stage this man felt tired of sacrificing so much to help these people, and he reduced his commitment. But it seemed as if the presence of the Holy Spirit in the meetings was not so real, and the number of conversions was slackening off too. This man decided that the Lord Jesus was worth it all, so he went back to his former sacrificial giving. Chapter 9:11 says, 'You will be made rich in every way so that you can be generous on every occasion, and through us your generosity will result in thanksgiving to God.' When we give out of sweet simplicity of spirit and out of love for Christ, as the Macedonians did, there will be many thanksgivings to God rebounding all around from people you would not expect.

The windows of heaven opened

Many Christians have stories to tell of how God has repaid them abundantly when they have been prepared to give sacrificially, fulfilling Jesus' instruction in Luke 6:38, 'Give, and it will be given to you. A good measure, pressed down, shaken together and running over...' Sometimes these things in the material world can show how much we really trust God. It is easy enough to say that we believe in God, but what about when it affects us in the physical realm?

There is a remarkable passage in Malachi where God issues us with a challenge to test him in the matter of material provision (Mal. 3:8-11). When we sacrifice that which we can see and touch and taste and feel, we show how much we are really prepared to lay all before him. The evil one will try to convince us that we will lose out, but as we follow the example of the Lord Jesus Christ who made himself poor for our sake, far from losing we will receive blessing. It may not be that we receive more money back than we give. We may be blessed with absence of expenses, answered prayers or fruitfulness in service. But over and over we have to come to the place of sacrifice afresh, where our generous Lord is able to release surprising blessings.

I know a minister who used to live in Mississippi, and because he had a large family, was from time to time in financial straits. During one such hard time, his wife surprised him with a suggestion about a month before Christmas. She said, 'Four missionaries to whom we give regular support have lost their last parent this year. Perhaps no one will remember them at Christmas. Why don't we send an extra cheque to help all four in time for Christmas?' Her husband replied, 'That is no doubt a worthy idea, but I don't see how we can afford it just now. Yes, I've paid all the bills for this month, including the tithe and missionary support, and there's barely enough to buy groceries for the rest of the month. If I send out four cheques – even modest ones – to those missionaries, it will drain out nearly all of our money for food. Nevertheless, if you really feel led to do it, and are willing to go short of food, I will go ahead and write the cheques.' She answered that they had extra potatoes and rice in the pantry and that therefore he should write the cheques.

The minister put four modest cheques in the post the next morning. When he returned home at the end of that day, his wife was away at music lessons with some of the children. However, he noticed an opened envelope on the kitchen table with his wife's handwriting across the front of it: 'See what the Lord has done!' He looked into the envelope and was amazed to find a cheque sent by a friend in another state, who knew nothing about his need. This cheque was a large one (for a humble minister). It was exactly one hundred times the combined amount he had posted to the missionaries that morning! (Then the happy minister had a sinful thought: 'What if I had given more?'!)

'Abuse never removes legitimate use'

A word of warning, however: we must beware of falling into the heresy of 'prosperity theology'. Our motive for giving is not so that we may receive back more. Nonetheless, Thomas Aquinas said that 'abuse never removes legitimate use.' Therefore we must not hold back the truth just because there are those who pervert the principle by promoting self-centred ministries that appeal to mercenary instincts. But on the contrary, we can help promote the true principle (legitimate use, not abuse) by quietly practising it ourselves, and by faithful expository preaching. Ultimately we give generously and encourage the saints to do so, because our God is generous. For example, in James 1:5 we read, 'If any of you lacks wisdom, he should ask God, who gives generously to all without finding fault, and it will be given to him.' The grammatical construction in the Greek uses the genitive absolute, so that a literal translation would read, 'let him ask of the Father because he is a giving God.' We see that our giving should be a response to the generous character of God himself, who pours himself out in love towards us, even though he has no obligation to give. The correct teaching of God's Word will emphasise that the laws of giving flow out of who the Lord Jesus Christ is and what he has done for us. May God encourage us to practise the law of the harvest ourselves first and teach these principles from God's Word, so that thanksgiving to God will redound all over our secular society. Could any investment advice be more valuable than that?

11

Bring Back the Flowers

2nd Corinthians 8:9

> [9]*For you know the grace of our Lord Jesus Christ, that though he was rich, yet for your sakes he became poor, so that you through his poverty might become rich.*

A very popular song amongst youth in the early1960s was 'Where have all the flowers gone?' Not infrequently one sees wilting 'flowers' that have lost their fragrance in Christian service. The vitality, thrill and sweetness are gone, and have been replaced by a sort of wooden professionalism. There may be a secret resentment at the cost of serving Christ by living for others, and a sullen refusal to think and live sacrificially. The orchids and the roses are gone! That is bad news in Christian life and ministry.

But the good news is this: it is only a short step to reclaiming the fragrance and beauty of a contagious Christian testimony! It comes back once again by a fresh and continuing look at the crucified One. As faith in 'the wondrous exchange' (as John Calvin calls it) is rekindled, we are surprised once again to find ourselves in the happy position of the hymnwriter:

Since my eyes were fixed on Jesus,
I've lost sight of all beside;
So enchained my spirit's vision,
Looking on the Crucified.

One of the reasons that Christian ministry and witness can begin to grind to a halt is simply that we forget how rich and majestic is the eternal Christ. Our hearts can begin to grow cold about the message, so we hold our chequebooks more tightly, guard our private time and seal our lips so we will not be thought odd in speaking of him. Maybe the gospel no longer moves or motivates us as it used to.

The riches of the Son

By way of remedy, Paul sets out in 8:9 the motivation, the method, the supernatural power and the glory of the Christian life and ministry: 'For you know the grace of our Lord Jesus Christ, that though he was rich, yet for your sakes he became poor, so that you through his poverty might become rich.' The *first* part of this verse says: 'though he was rich'. I once read this verse to a children's Bible class and asked them, 'When was the Lord Jesus Christ rich? He didn't own a home during his life. He died a shameful, terrible death before he was buried in a borrowed tomb. When was he rich?' One of the children had it right when he said, 'He was rich before he came to earth.'

We are told in the prologue to John's Gospel that 'In the beginning was the Word', clearly identified as Christ, the Second Person of the Trinity and the eternal Son of the Father. 'In the beginning was the Word, and the Word was with God, and the Word was God' (John 1:1). Christ was always God. The whole idea of family life comes out of the Trinity. That is why we are made and structured to want to live in a family as an analogy of the love relationship within the Godhead. The love of human parents and children reflects God's essential nature, but there are great differences as well. One of the contrasts is that, whereas human parents are always a different generation from their children, within the blessed Holy Trinity the Son is every bit as old as the Father. Athanasius said that the Father has never been without his Son, or without the Holy Spirit linking Father and Son eternally together. That is who the Lord Jesus Christ, the Second Person of the Trinity, was before he came into this world. We are told also in John's Gospel that 'Through him all things were made; without him nothing was made that has been made' (John 1:3). Everything in heaven and earth has been created through the agency of the Second Person of the Trinity. All beauty, light, joy, glory, refreshment, everything that is desirable was made through him, including the very angels of heaven. There is a hymn that says:

> Heaven's arches rang when the angels sang,
> Proclaiming thy royal degree;
> But in lowly birth didst thou come to earth,
> And in great humility.

The poverty of the Son

The *second* part of verse 9 says: 'yet for your sakes he became poor'. One of the early theologians of the Church, Hilary of Poitiers in France, wrote in about 350 AD, concerning the impoverishment of the Second Person of the Trinity:

> What worthy return can we make for so great a condescension? The one, only begotten God, ineffably born of God, entered the virgin's womb and grew and took the frame of poor humanity. He who upholds the universe, within whom and through whom are all things, was brought forth by common childbirth. He at whose voice archangels and angels tremble and heaven and earth and all the elements of this world are melted, was heard in childish wailing. The invisible and incomprehensible whom sight and feeling and touch cannot gauge was wrapped in a cradle. We were raised because

> He was lowered. Shame to Him was glory to us. He being God made flesh His residence and in return we are lifted anew from the flesh to God.

A slug on the garden path

When the Lord Jesus Christ, the Second Person of the Trinity, entered into this created order and became a creature, he lowered himself to become a human being like us in every way and yet without sin. The Creator enters the creation while still remaining God, becoming God and man in one person. Some theologians would argue that this is a greater miracle than the creation of the cosmos out of nothing. C S Lewis said that the condescension of Christ in leaving the courts of heaven and coming down to be born of a poor Jewish maiden is a far greater lowering than if you or I could be reduced to a slug on the garden path. An old gospel hymn says:

> O the love that drew salvation's plan,
> O the mighty gulf that God did span,
> O the love that brought it down to man, at Calvary.

The eternal Son of God knew increasing humiliation and impoverishment throughout his life on earth. He was born into an honourable but poor and obscure family in a downtrodden country. He grew up working with his hands as a carpenter, and when he entered his public ministry at the Levitical age of thirty, he would have had very little means of support as an itinerant preacher. We understand from the Gospel of Luke that Jesus was financially maintained in large measure by the donations of a number of women whose hearts God had touched. He never had a home of his own as far as we know, although he loved to visit the home of Mary, Martha and Lazarus at Bethany. Their house was like a home to him, but he did not own it. To the best of our knowledge he had no impressive clothing, and not even the money to pay his taxes. When he was required to pay tax, it was provided through Peter's catch of a fish with a coin in its mouth. At one time he said, 'Foxes have holes and birds of the air have nests, but the Son of Man has nowhere to lay his head' (Luke 9:58).

Besmirched with our sin

The poverty that Jesus experienced is intensified to the point of absolute humiliation in the last week of his life. He will become totally identified with the lot of all sinners who will ever believe in him. God sends his Son to take our humanity, to fulfil the covenant that Adam failed to keep, to love and obey the Father with filial devotion as we have never done. He goes down deeper than any of us could ever go, identifying himself with our dereliction and torment. We catch a glimpse of this in the Garden of Gethsemane, where Hebrews 5:7 tells us that Jesus offered up loud cries and tears.

The great devotional writer William Law asked why the Saviour requested the inner circle of the disciples to stay awake and to pray with him. Some of the answers given to that question have been superficial: for example, the suggestion that it is to teach us to stay awake and pray with troubled people. Although no doubt true, such an explanation is inadequate to the situation. William Law suggests that Jesus is beginning to become so identified with human sin that the sorrows of a lost soul in hell are now beginning to open up within the Redeemer's consciousness. But the inner circle of the disciples go to sleep, leaving him to his solitary suffering. We see him sweating great drops of blood, so intense is the agony not merely in contemplating the physical sufferings of the crucifixion, but far more the horror of having his holy soul besmirched with the sin of humanity. We cannot begin to imagine what a torture it would be for one whose pure mind had never entertained an evil thought, to be filled with human wickedness.

One of the objections we hear most often is this: 'If God is a God of love, why is it that he would insist on the punishment of sin?

Why is it a loving God would have a hell for people whose sins are allegedly not forgiven to go to? Is that consistent with the God of love we are told about in the Bible?' But here is the answer: what is meant by love? Many people will even use the word 'love' to excuse immoral behaviour and to avoid their obligations to God and to others. Thus they deny the moral character of the God of love.

We have to get our definition of love not from humanism or some other religion, and not out of our own heads, but out of Scripture as God's own Word. There we will find love in its balance, its truth, its fullness and its reality, not something we have invented or redefined. The Bible teaches that God's love has a character to it that defines it. It is the most tender, profound, self-sacrificial, giving love, but it is also pure and holy. By contrast, sin is a cancer that would devour the universe and eat God off his throne if it were allowed to go its full course. If God were to fail to punish evil in a moral universe that he has made himself along the lines of his own character, God would deny himself and everything would pass into non-existence. God's holy love requires him to deal adequately and victoriously with the destructive monster of sin.

Infinite love

The liberal German theology espoused by Albert Schweitzer, which is still influential within the intellectual circles of Protestantism, gives the impression that Jesus was a good and well-meaning person, who lost control of the situation and died as a result. Sadly, evil was too strong for him to handle, and he died as a broken and disillusioned man, but his spirit of love and forgiveness lives on in some way leaving us an honourable example. This is the precise opposite of what the New Testament teaches us.

Consider the scene described in John 18:3-6: a group of soldiers armed with spears and swords surrounds this broken, impoverished-looking man with tear-stained cheeks and blood already coming out of the pores of his skin. When one of the officers asks him 'Who are you?', Jesus uses the divine name 'I am' or 'Yahweh' given to Moses in Exodus 3:14. Those soldiers, who think they are so strong and well-equipped, are knocked flat on their faces in the dirt. It is as though a beam of the uncreated light breaks into the darkness of the Judean night. It is as though a surge of deity rushes through the manhood of our Lord; this is not merely a broken, humble man whom evil is defeating, but this is the One who sits enthroned with deity, the fellow of Jehovah, the Ancient of Days. Jesus is in charge of the whole situation, and his impoverishment is totally voluntary, arising out of his infinite love for us. In John 10:17-18 Jesus says, 'I lay down my life – only to take it up again. No-one takes it from me, but I lay it down of my own accord. I have authority to lay it down and authority to take it up again.'

Given that Jesus was completely in control of the situation, how amazing it is that he voluntarily underwent such abuse and agony. He was beaten on his back with a Roman whip that had nine leather thongs studded with metal or pottery shards that would have torn his flesh. He was mocked, spat upon and finally led up to Calvary to be crucified, when he became totally identified with all the sins of all the people who will ever believe. Philippians 2:5-11 tells us that 'He humbled himself and became obedient to death – even death on a cross!' When God the Son cries out to God the Father from Psalm 22:1: 'Eloi, Eloi, lama sabachthani? My God, My God, why have you forsaken me?' something happened that we will never fully understand. Martin Luther asked: 'How can it be? God forsaken by God?' It is as if the loving Father has to turn away his face from the Son he loves supremely, because the Father cannot look upon the evil which now resides, as it were, in the Son.

As far as we know, the first written sermon preserved from the early Christian church and rediscovered in the early twentieth century, was preached at Easter 169 AD by a man called Melito of Sardis. It contains this profound statement about the sufferings of Christ:

> 'How can it be? He who fixed the sun and the moon and the planets in their places is now fixed on the cross? He who hung the lights in the sky now hangs on a tree. He from whose hand first flowed in creative power all the streams and the rivers and the very oceans of this world; now the roof of His mouth is so parched and dry that He cries out "I thirst".'

According to John Calvin's interpretation, Christ suffered the very pains of hell on the cross, so infinitely deep and horrible was the sea of grief and humiliation as he passed through the outer darkness of being forsaken by God. Wonderfully though, Jesus did not die to stay dead; as the late James S Stewart once said: 'When death took on Jesus of Nazareth it took on too much.'

Infinite wealth from the Son

The *third* part of 2 Corinthians 8:9 gives the results: 'so that you through his poverty might become rich'. Because he was the innocent Holy One, his vicarious, substitutionary sufferings more than repay all that the holy righteousness of God would ever require for a sinner to be forgiven. A famous Presbyterian preacher in Philadelphia a number of years ago, Donald Gray Barnhouse, used to say: 'Your sins can be in only one of two places. They can either remain on your own head, in which case you have the eternal problem of a finite soul bearing infinite guilt which can never be taken away. Alternatively, your sins can be taken off your head and placed on the head of the Redeemer who has more than paid all God's holy requirements for your pardon.' You can be forgiven, endowed with newness of life and restored to the fellowship of the One whom you were made to love in an eternity of bliss. That is how wealthy we have become.

All who will identify with the Lord Jesus through faith can have the past totally wiped clean. Never can a thing be raised against you that would keep you out of the gates of heaven, out of the inner chambers of the Father's house of light. The work of Jesus Christ can be illustrated by the incident in Exodus 7:8-12 where Moses threw down his rod before Pharaoh and it turned into a snake. Pharaoh's magicians were able to copy this, but their snakes were devoured by the snake of Moses. It is as if the death and resurrection of Jesus swallows up all of our deaths.

The 'bee' that has lost its sting

In 1 Corinthians 15:55, the great resurrection chapter, Paul asks this remarkable question: 'Where, O Death, is your sting?' By way of illustration, a honey bee can only sting you one time. It will leave its stinger in the flesh of the first person it stings, and after a few hours the bee will die. A honey bee that has stung someone else can buzz around you and scare you, but it no longer has the power to deposit a sting with poison inside of you. Death has left its sting in the Redeemer; all the poison that death could ever deposit in us has been drained off in the Lord Jesus Christ. When those who trust in Christ face the end of their earthly life, death can only buzz around us and maybe scare us a little bit, but it has no power to hurt us. Part of the wealth we have in Christ is that we no longer have death to fear. Hebrews 2:14-15 says, 'Since the children have flesh and blood, he too shared in their humanity so that by his death he might destroy him who holds the power of death – that is, the devil – and free those who all their lives were held in slavery by their fear of death.'

These are the riches available to us through the impoverishment of our Lord Jesus Christ: forgiveness of sin, abundant life, eternal joy, meaning and purpose, guidance for living, victory over death, and fellowship with God. This is the message and the method by which the church may retake our culture, if God so wills. Many aspects of our methodology are fluid and can be adapted to the times, but we must keep to the essential message revealed in Scripture. We must not set up church services based only on people's 'felt needs', because often they are not the real or the most important needs. The church may be looking for better methods to get greater numbers, but God is looking for better people. As Christian people we need to be so taken up in appreciation of and devotion to this Saviour who became poor to enrich us, that we would do something of the same in our own limited capacities, offering up ourselves to the service of the Lord Jesus Christ for the benefit of others and the glory of God. In this position, the fragrance and sweetness of the 'Lily of the Valley' and the 'Rose of Sharon' comes back upon us and spreads in many directions, little though we may be aware of it, for we are taken up with him and with pointing others to the source of all blessing. Then, with Josiah Conder, we can sing aloud:

> Throughout the universe of bliss
> The centre Thou, and sun,
> The eternal theme of praise is this,
> To heaven's beloved one:
> Worthy, O Lamb of God, art Thou,
> That every knee to Thee should bow!

12

Criticism of Ministers

2 Corinthians 10

*[1]By the meekness and gentleness of Christ, I appeal to you—I, Paul,
who am "timid" when face to face with you, but "bold" when away! [2]I
beg you that when I come I may not have to be as bold as I expect to
be toward some people who think that we live by the standards of this
world. [3]For though we live in the world, we do not wage war as the
world does. [4]The weapons we fight with are not the weapons of the
world. On the contrary, they have divine power to demolish strong-
holds. [5]We demolish arguments and every pretension that sets itself
up against the knowledge of God, and we take captive every thought
to make it obedient to Christ. [6]And we will be ready to punish every
act of disobedience, once your obedience is complete.*

*[7]You are looking only on the surface of things. If anyone is con-
fident that he belongs to Christ, he should consider again that we
belong to Christ just as much as he. [8]For even if I boast somewhat
freely about the authority the Lord gave us for building you up rather
than pulling you down, I will not be ashamed of it. [9]I do not want to*

seem to be trying to frighten you with my letters. [10]*For some say, "His letters are weighty and forceful, but in person he is unimpressive and his speaking amounts to nothing."* [11]*Such people should realize that what we are in our letters when we are absent, we will be in our actions when we are present.*

[12]*We do not dare to classify or compare ourselves with some who commend themselves. When they measure themselves by themselves and compare themselves with themselves, they are not wise.* [13]*We, however, will not boast beyond proper limits, but will confine our boasting to the field God has assigned to us, a field that reaches even to you.* [14]*We are not going too far in our boasting, as would be the case if we had not come to you, for we did get as far as you with the gospel of Christ.* [15]*Neither do we go beyond our limits by boasting of work done by others. Our hope is that, as your faith continues to grow, our area of activity among you will greatly expand,* [16]*so that we can preach the gospel in the regions beyond you. For we do not want to boast about work already done in another man's territory.* [17]*But, "Let him who boasts boast in the Lord."* [18]*For it is not the one who commends himself who is approved, but the one whom the Lord commends.*

An elderly cousin of mine was a country doctor in eastern North Carolina for sixty years. On the wall of his surgery hung this plaque: 'In order to avoid criticism: say nothing, do nothing, be nothing.' Along with most ministerial salaries comes the added bonus of free criticism: some of it loving and helpful, and some of it mean-spirited and untrue. How does a servant of Christ handle criticism without becoming either hard-hearted and unapproachable, or else so supinely sensitive that he is all but paralysed into 'saying nothing, doing nothing and being nothing'?

2 Corinthians 10 answers this question so crucial to every Christian ministry. In this tenth chapter Paul is writing about how the truth of the gospel is communicated through individual human

personalities filled with the Holy Spirit to people who do not know God, and who may resent those who do. Before we can do real good to others, we must first face the ultimate question that God would have us pose to ourselves. The biggest question of time and eternity that any human being could ever face is: 'What do you think of Jesus Christ?' Once that all-determining question is answered, then the believer will operate his daily life on the basis of another big question: 'What do we think of ourselves in Christ?' Since by grace I am alive in him for evermore, what do the particularities of my existence really mean? In other words, how do we come to terms with the way the Lord has made us – most importantly through grace – but also through our genetic inheritance and our environment?

None of us can be sure how much of our personality is due to our genes and how much due to our upbringing. It seems likely that God works through both to create the potential of the person he has allowed us to be, as he brings us into 'the world of grace' (to quote William Still). Answering these questions is basic to all fruitful Christian service, for the question of our identity in Christ will assume great importance over the years, especially as we encounter challenges to our message or our leadership. There will be very few people who are honest enough to say, 'I don't like your message, I don't like to submit to this God. Yes, what you're saying is in the Bible. But I reject the Bible because I don't want God's authority over my life.' A thoroughly honest person like that is more likely to be found outside the church. But generally in the church they will not say, 'I hate this gospel that you're preaching.' So if they cannot get at God himself, the next best thing is to get at you. Maybe you will face criticism of your appearance, personal characteristics or preaching style. Sometimes criticism is valid and needs to be acted on, if we are to be fruitful.

Although we must be open to questioning the way we do things, still we must not take it too personally. As we think and pray about it, we may be aware that the pressure of the Word of God is affecting those who criticise. Be patient with them, for sometimes the debate will move on to the message, and there may be a real opportunity for conversion, or there may be some area where critics have helped you improve. Certainly I have been refined by valid criticism, painful though it was. But here let us think about unfair and destructive criticism. There are seasons of attack in any Christian ministry; as we pass through the battles, the pressure may lessen. But we never know when it will break out again, which is one of the reasons why it is so very important to be reminding ourselves of who we are in the light of the providence of God in grace and in our own background and life experience.

The problem

In chapter 10 we see first Paul's problem, and secondly Paul's solution. *First, the criticisms that Paul faced* from people who were challenging his spiritual leadership. In verse 1 he is obviously quoting remarks that some of them are reported as making about him, namely that he does not look impressive. The Gnostic gospels contain a physical description of Paul that is somewhat unflattering, although the reliability of such sources is open to question. In the classical Hellenistic world, much as in our culture, great importance was attached to sport, fitness and physical impressiveness. There were influential schools of rhetoric where the skills of polished oratory were taught.

Like much contemporary political debate, the substance of what was said was often ignored in favour of a speaker's appearance or fluency. Paul tells the Corinthian Christians in verse 7a, 'You are looking only on the surface of things.' From verse 10 we deduce that Paul's critics were saying, 'Yes, he can write a good letter but his bodily presence is weak and his speech contemptible.' They attacked him for physical things because they did not like his message, and they wanted to wield power in the church themselves, without having to submit to a costly, unpopular message. Yes, when you have humans as ministers, there is always a necessary place for fair criticism. But this was unfair and unworthily motivated. How do we deal with that?

The solution

So, *in the second place, Paul's solution*, or rather God's solution for Paul and for me and for you is given. The first thing we note in verse 7b, is that the apostle Paul knows what he is worth to God, when he says, 'we belong to Christ.' This is the core of our identity: we are clothed in his spotless robes of righteousness. He took our sins away on Calvary's cross, and his blood has cleansed us. If the devil can get us to focus on ourselves he can certainly stop us from praying because then we say to ourselves, 'Remember what you said, remember the nasty thoughts you had, remember that doubt, remember this weakness. You'd better reform yourself before you pray.' If we focus on ourselves and our performance we will seldom feel able to pray with any expectation. We need to focus on our identity in Christ according to the Word of God.

When we are identified with the Lord Jesus Christ through the Holy Spirit, God looks upon us as being in his Son. So when we pray it is as if the Father hears the beloved tones of the Son breaking through our prayers. If we knew the power we have because we are praying in union with Christ, we could not keep away from prayer. Paul the apostle knows how much he is worth to God, not because of his deeds, but because he has been chosen in Christ. He knows essentially who he is and to whom he belongs, and this is the solution to the criticism he faces.

Thomas Aquinas wrote more than fifty theological volumes, but towards the end of his life he had some kind of a vision or special experience of God. He appears to have died trusting in the merits of Christ, not proud of his own amazing writings. Similarly, in verses 4-5, the apostle Paul bases his thinking not on his own abilities (or lack of physical prowess either), but on the word of Christ. He is talking about the weapons with which we must fight as God calls us into battle. The New Testament so often speaks in military terms. When it speaks of our going out into this culture, we go as soldiers of the cross. Ephesians 6:13-17 describes the whole armour of God. We must resist the devil who goes about, says Peter, as a roaring lion seeking whom he may devour. James 4:7 says, 'Resist the devil, and he will flee from you.' We are fighting from a position of imparted victory, but we still have to fight and take the risks, using the tactics Paul describes in verse 5.

Engaging in the conflict

First, Paul says, 'We demolish arguments and every pretension that sets itself up against the knowledge of God...' Secular culture, whether classical, modern or post-modern, exalts itself against the knowledge of God, as it seeks to promote a different kind of knowledge. It is often said that the ultra-liberal mind is very tolerant of everything except evangelical Christianity. In the USA recently a person who suggested that sexual abstinence before marriage was something that God wanted, was taken to court on the basis that bringing religion into education should not be allowed in the state school of a free republic.

Part of post-modernism is a denial of the very possibility of real objective knowledge, especially when it comes to moral absolutes. In order to avoid facing God, some of the post-modernists go so far as to maintain that human beings cannot know anything. But presumably they think at least they know that much! And if they admit one piece of knowledge, why not others?

The apostle Paul would label such claims 'pretensions'. Looking Jesus Christ in the face is the way to demolish such shoddy arguments and puffed-up pretensions. Lack of clear contact with reality leaves us prey to the demons of our culture, whereas knowledge of God in the face of Christ is the basis of every other true knowledge (both of self and the world around us) and is the ground of liberation from fear of the world and control by its attitudes.

Surrendering to our Captain

Secondly, Paul says 'we take captive every thought', using another military analogy, that of the hostage. Although the word normally has negative connotations, here it is used positively in the sense of letting the Lord Jesus Christ capture our thoughts, as in the hymn line 'Make me a captive, Lord, and then I shall be free.'

In our relativistic culture it is not that there is no god, but it is a different god. Either it will be self or some aspect of the culture set up as an idol. By contrast those who have their thoughts taken captive by Christ will know their identity in him, and thus know the true and living God. In the light of this knowledge, the apostle Paul refuses to judge himself or let others judge him on the false basis of the world's values. He will only be assessed on the basis of his value in and to Christ.

Here is the danger in some 'trendy' ministerial seminars which teach ministers techniques on how to make a better impression on the public. Of course, there is no harm in correcting irritating mannerisms or unthoughtful habits; indeed we must do so. But when it comes to advising ministers to buy more expensive suits than their business acquaintances in order to impress, then the agenda is being set by a superficial world. Letting the culture set the trend for the church, and in this case for its ministers, entails abandoning the one resource we really need: a fresh touch of our true life, which is 'hidden with Christ in God'. (And, by the way, propriety in personal appearance and bearing will be encouraged, not discouraged, by every new meeting of grace with the Lord Jesus.)

Constantly focusing on our identity in the risen Lord, rather than wasting energy in the attempt to keep abreast of ever-shifting cultural styles, trends and opinions is part of the battle we wage to bring every thought into captivity to Christ. This is not a barbarian negation of human culture, but rather a thoughtful subjugation of it to something higher. It is precisely in this well-thought-out subjugation of the lower to the higher that the servant of God finds liberty of spirit and the ability to handle criticism and controversy responsibly.

For instance, Paul realises that God has made him what he is, with both strengths and limitations. He is aware of the advantages of his background: from the tribe of Benjamin, well schooled by the best teacher, Gamaliel, an exemplary Pharisee and a free citizen of Rome. Nevertheless now, as a Christian believer, he takes no pride in his privileged upbringing, but describes it as 'dung' (to translate literally the indelicate actual Greek word) compared with knowing Christ and the power of his resurrection.

One of the greatest signs of Christian maturity is the ability to accept the way God, in his providence, has made us with both positive and negative aspects in our lives and personalities, along with a growing freedom from the need to impress people. Some people seem to have difficulty in accepting who they are, and are always trying to be someone else, or striving to copy another's success so as to make a better impression, or perhaps disarm potential criticism. This can block the light of the Lord Jesus from shining through the personality that he gave us, and makes us unduly focus on either praise or blame, rather than on the true needs of the persons with whom we are interacting. In order to focus on the needs of others, we need liberation from self, which flows from accepting ourselves in Christ. Can we accept our strengths and weaknesses as being in the plan of God? Can we accept an unpleasant situation or corrupt culture in which he has placed us as being part of his plan?

God uses our weaknesses

In Exodus chapters 3 and 4, Moses is called by God to do a humanly impossible task in leading all those slaves out of their captivity under the world's greatest military power. Verse 10 of chapter 4 says: 'Moses said to the Lord, "Lord, I have never been eloquent, neither in the past nor since you have spoken to your servant. I am slow of speech and tongue."' Notice that God did not say, 'Well, son, that isn't true, you really are an impressive speaker, you have an excellent voice.' The Lord evidently concurs that he is slow of speech and tongue, but that is not the problem. 'The Lord said to him, "Who gave man his mouth? Who makes him deaf or mute? Who gives him sight or makes him blind? Is it not I, the Lord? Now go; I will help you speak and will teach you what to say"' (vv. 11-12). This is something we need to accept at the deepest level of our life: the providence of a loving and wise God in using the weaknesses of our background and our current difficulties, as well as our strong points, to enable us to be of service to him as we are liberated by this aspect of true faith to focus on helping others, rather than on worrying about self and how positively or negatively they evaluate us. Oh for the grace to help people, rather than impress them!

Real-life testimonies

The following situations are three real-life examples of Christian people who accepted that God in his providence could use them in their difficult circumstances, and in so doing, led their thoughts into captivity to Christ, by which they were liberated in spirit and set free to serve. One minister and his wife were told that their unborn child had spina bifida, and were asked whether they wanted to have an abortion. They explained that they could not do that because of their Christian faith. This happened to them twice. It has at times been painful and very demanding on them, as their children require much special care. But long ago they came through to an acceptance that the all-powerful, all-loving God is in control, and they have a remarkable and unobtrusive testimony as they quietly maintain a surprisingly normal, loving and cheerful home. Indeed, they consider themselves very privileged to have three remarkable children (one with no health problems and two with spina bifida). They have been taking every thought hostage, captive to the obedience of Christ. They would not be aware of it, but glory has shone out from them to an entire community and far beyond.

Donald Gray Barnhouse, of Tenth Presbyterian Church in Philadelphia, tells the story of a young pastor he knew whose wife gave birth to a baby boy with Down's Syndrome. Dr Barnhouse took his Bible, rushed right up to the hospital to see them and read this very passage from Exodus 4:11, '"Who gave man his mouth? Who makes him deaf or mute? Who gives him sight or makes him blind? Is it not I, the Lord?"' He said, 'This baby is God's special gift to you. This is providence that it should have happened, and it is a way that God's grace will work more deeply in your lives and through your ministry. Offer up this baby to God. Trust in the God who gave his Son for you and he will multiply your ministry as you submit to this hard providence as some way being in his love.' The head nurse at the hospital was a sceptic, who did not go to church and was really resentful of ministers who kept coming on cheery visits to patients. This nursing sister went in to talk to the couple, expecting them to be devastated and maybe embittered. The young pastor quoted this verse and said, 'God has given us a very special gift. It's this baby. We thank him for it.' The nursing sister was absolutely broken open; she had never heard such a thing in her life. On Sunday morning she was at that young minister's church together with thirty other nurses, of whom twenty-five were eventually converted including that nursing sister. This young minister and his wife were able to accept their situation as part of God's providence. Thereupon, their influence for good became very wide.

William Hill of Virginia was a very effective evangelist with a brilliant mind. He had contracted polio when he was a boy, which had left his body severely twisted. As a teenager he had become very embittered against God, asking himself what kind of God could let him look like this? Somehow the grace of God broke through to him, and he was able to say, 'Lord, I may not be much but what I am you can have – all of it, absolutely all of it. I do believe Jesus loved me and gave himself for me and he is worthy of what little I've got.' He became one of the finest, most faithful, anointed preachers, mightily used by God to bring countless numbers of souls into the kingdom. His concern over how he looked was replaced by a heart of love for others. Happy exchange!

You might say, 'How can you bear it, how can you accept these things?' God is not the author of sin, so biblical thinking does not blame God for the evil in it, yet in his wise providence he allowed it. Surely he could have stopped it? How do you bear up and keep loving God, submitting to him and trusting him when tragedy hits your family? How do you accept the things you do not like about yourself? How can we help the people in our churches come to terms with the deep hurts they may have experienced?

The key is found in Romans 8:32: 'He who did not spare his own Son, but gave him up for us all – how will he not also, along with him, graciously give us all things?' Surely if our heavenly Father gave up the most precious thing to him – his holy, perfect Son for people such as we are, to be abused and ultimately slain on the cross – the Father loves us so much that we can trust him when precious things are removed from us or are never given to us. When we do not understand we do not ask him to explain; we know he is worthy to be trusted because of the infinite love he has shown us when he gave us the very Son of his heart. This is surely part of what Paul means by taking 'captive every thought to make it obedient to Christ'.

Some of the writings of Alexander Whyte, late minister of Saint George's West Church, Edinburgh, help us marshall, our thoughts into this glorious captivity. Especially his essay on 'Our Lord's Favourite Graces' is of help when we feel we have a cruel yoke and a heavy burden and are perhaps looking at them more than at our Lord. He says:

> Go to Christ and tell Him that as His cross on the way to Calvary crushed Him, so your cross, your burden and your yoke will not be long in crushing you into the grave unless you get help from Him to bear all these things. He may possibly remove your burden altogether if you are importunate enough. He can wholly remove it if that seems good in His sight. On the other hand, who knows? He may have such a plot in His divine counsels concerning you that he may

> say to you that His grace is sufficient for you and that His strength is to be made perfect in your weakness. Go to Him in any case and whatever He sees it good to do with you and your burden, He will at any rate begin to give you another heart under it. He will begin to give you what His Father gave Him. He will give you, burden or no burden, a meek and lowly heart. A truly meek and lowly heart will enable you to carry ten burdens as big as yours and ten yokes as galling as yours, and that to the end of your days on earth. It is not your burden that so weighs you down. It is your proud, rebellious, self-seeking, self-pleasing heart. Once make yourself a new heart and the thing is done. From that day your yoke will be easy and your burden light. Just try for one thing to see yourself as you really are. Just try to look at yourself continually as Christ looked at Himself. You have not reflected enough on a thousand good reasons that God must have for the way He is yoking you and loading you. 'Come unto me', says the patient burden-bearer, 'Put on my meek mind, enter into my lowly heart, imitate me.' Go home and speak the mild and meek word where you have been wont to speak the high and hard word and thus to exasperate your own yoke and the yokes of others. Hold your peace. Do not speak at all about things concerning which you have been wont to speak about so unadvisedly and so bitterly. Kneel down in secret at His feet and refuse to rise till your yoke is either lightened or your heart is strengthened.

He goes on to mention Samuel Rutherford, who in one of his golden letters, writes of: 'a cross that had such wings that they bore up both the cross itself and the bearer of that cross'. Dr Whyte then adds:

> Your yoke also will sprout wings if you come sufficiently close to Christ with it and continue to consult Him about it and about yourself under it. Take courage and come to Him for He is as meek and lowly-minded, as accessible and affable in heaven as ever he was on earth, more so if that were possible. Though He be high, He is not any more high-minded than ever He was, as you will live to testify and tell, if only you will take your case to Him.

Focus on the heart of God

This is what the apostle Paul did, as he brought every matter before the Lord. The important thing is not how impressive an image we can project, nor how large a circle of influence we seem to have, because we can never know that anyway. Nor does it matter that we please everybody. The vital need is for us to trust the Lord in the midst of whatever situation is bothering us, whether it is the way he made us, or the circumstances in which we find ourselves, including the shifting attitudes of others towards us. Our need is to focus again on the heart of God revealed in the face of our Lord Jesus. Then, like Paul, we give the situation into the loving hands of our Lord, taking every thought into captivity to the One who gave us his all. He then frees us to serve our generation.

The more the servants of Christ do this, the less they are shaken by harsh criticism or inflated with fulsome praise. Appropriating ever anew who they are in Christ, they are set free to be perceptive and available to the spiritual needs of busy and frustrated votaries of an empty world system. This is God's appointed way for us to help people get off a useless merry-go-round that leaves their whirling lives accomplishing nothing, and themselves being nothing. It shows them that everything worth having is in Christ, and that by grace it can be theirs, as well as ours.

13

The Agony and the Ecstasy

2 Corinthians 12

1I must go on boasting. Although there is nothing to be gained, I will
go on to visions and revelations from the Lord. 2I know a man in
Christ who fourteen years ago was caught up to the third heaven.
Whether it was in the body or out of the body I do not know—God
knows. 3And I know that this man—whether in the body or apart
from the body I do not know, but God knows— 4was caught up to
paradise. He heard inexpressible things, things that man is not per-
mitted to tell. 5I will boast about a man like that, but I will not boast
about myself, except about my weaknesses. 6Even if I should choose to
boast, I would not be a fool, because I would be speaking the truth.
But I refrain, so no one will think more of me than is warranted by
what I do or say.

7To keep me from becoming conceited because of these surpass-
ingly great revelations, there was given me a thorn in my flesh, a
messenger of Satan, to torment me. 8Three times I pleaded with the
Lord to take it away from me. 9But he said to me, "My grace is suffi-

cient for you, for my power is made perfect in weakness." Therefore I will boast all the more gladly about my weaknesses, so that Christ's power may rest on me. [10]That is why, for Christ's sake, I delight in weaknesses, in insults, in hardships, in persecutions, in difficulties. For when I am weak, then I am strong.

I have made a fool of myself, but you drove me to it. I ought to have been commended by you, for I am not in the least inferior to the "super-apostles," even though I am nothing. [12]The things that mark an apostle—signs, wonders and miracles—were done among you with great perseverance. [13]How were you inferior to the other churches, except that I was never a burden to you? Forgive me this wrong!

[14]Now I am ready to visit you for the third time, and I will not be a burden to you, because what I want is not your possessions but you. After all, children should not have to save up for their parents, but parents for their children. [15]So I will very gladly spend for you everything I have and expend myself as well. If I love you more, will you love me less? [16]Be that as it may, I have not been a burden to you. Yet, crafty fellow that I am, I caught you by trickery! [17]Did I exploit you through any of the men I sent you? [18]I urged Titus to go to you and I sent our brother with him. Titus did not exploit you, did he? Did we not act in the same spirit and follow the same course?

[19]Have you been thinking all along that we have been defending ourselves to you? We have been speaking in the sight of God as those in Christ; and everything we do, dear friends, is for your strengthening. [20]For I am afraid that when I come I may not find you as I want you to be, and you may not find me as you want me to be. I fear that there may be quarreling, jealousy, outbursts of anger, factions, slander, gossip, arrogance and disorder. [21]I am afraid that when I come again my God will humble me before you, and I will be grieved over many who have sinned earlier and have not repented of the impurity, sexual sin and debauchery in which they have indulged.

Some forty years ago a famous biography of the superb Renaissance artist, Michelangelo, was published. Its title captures Paul's summary of the fruitful Christian ministry: *The Agony and the Ecstasy*.

In 2 Corinthians chapter 12, the apostle Paul writes about two facets of Christian ministry that always go together when the church is reaching out to bring men and women into the kingdom of God. On the one hand there is painful pressure and costly suffering; on the other there is transcendent power and transforming glory. Paul is writing about this agony and ecstasy in chapters 11, 12 and 13, as he brings to a close this treatise on gospel ministry in a dying culture. We might summarise this paradox of suffering and glory by two mysterious images that Paul describes with a certain reserve. On the one hand the thorn in the flesh that God declined to take away from him, and on the other hand the experience of being caught up into the glory of heaven, where he saw wonders that he was not allowed to express in human language. The suffering and the glory always go together in a fruitful Christian life.

Because of our lack of balance through the fall of Adam that infected us all, we would like to have the glory without the suffering. There are forms of Christianity today that attempt to offer you Christianity without a cross. That is not authentic, biblical Christianity and it has no power to change people. On the other hand you can go to the other extreme of having a defeatist mentality – a cross without the empty tomb of the resurrected Christ. Authentic biblical Christianity holds together the pain of the many crosses that we may be called upon to bear, and the glory of knowing the presence of God which far outweighs the cost. The cross and the crown are intertwined in a God-given balance; if the church tries to separate them it will wither and die, and lose all influence on the culture.

The first five verses of chapter 12 deal with the glory, while verses 6-19 deal with the painful cost. This is the reversed order of what we might expect. Normally, the church remembers the crucifixion on Good Friday before it celebrates the resurrection on Easter Sunday. Both in chapters 5 and 12, Paul's reversal has theological significance. He is saying that the Lord never puts a cross on you and me to bear, except as one who is already risen with Christ and is seated with him in the heavenly realms. It is those people who have already been resurrected spiritually with the Lord Jesus, to whom God says, 'I'm going to ask you to trust me, love me and submit to me even though it hurts, so that I can use you.' This is how God reaches men and women in our truth-denying culture.

The glory

First, in verses 1-5 *Paul writes of the glory*. We are told in John's Gospel that Jesus Christ is the glory of the Father, the very character of God, seen in the flesh. He is now in the heavenly world in the source of the glory, although we see some of that glory shining out as the Holy Spirit works in the believers. Paul seems to have had the experience of being caught up into that glory-world in heaven, although he does not know whether it was in the body or in the spirit. God let a human being see into heaven before death, for Paul would live for many years after this. What Paul saw was so wonderful and ineffable that he cannot describe it in words.

Jonathan Edwards' book *Charity and its Fruits* has a wonderful last chapter entitled, 'Heaven – a World of Love'. It is the fountainhead of all that is worth having, the final reality of the things we desire the most to have on earth. We might be tempted to say, 'Have I got to leave earth and give up these things? Home, family, the hills where I was raised, or these love relationships, or the very flowers, the clouds, the mountains, the sea? Have I got to leave all this?' C S Lewis points out that when we get to heaven we will then understand that the only reason we loved these things on earth was because they were just little reflections of what is in the glory-world.

God does not say a great deal about the beauties of heaven, although we know it is a wonderful place above all our desiring.

Paul is not allowed to say too much about what he saw, perhaps because we are not ready for such knowledge. God would have us not concentrate so much on heaven and its glories, although it is proper to think of it and be encouraged by it. Instead, God would have us concentrate on himself and especially on his Son, so we must walk by faith and keep our eyes on him. Christ is our captain and our guiding star, and he will get us to our destination. Thus Paul will be speaking a great deal more about Christ, the significance of his sufferings, his resurrection, the coming of his Spirit, our union with him and our service for him, than he will of the glory itself.

The current interest in people who claim to have had 'out-of-the-body, near-death experiences' raises questions as to why they have so much to say about it when the apostle Paul was so restrained. Perhaps if God showed us too much of the glory ahead we might be restless and find it too difficult to stay here on earth. So the Lord wants you to be content here, to be grateful to be on earth until he gets you ready to go to glory, which will surely be soon enough.

It is interesting that at the end of 1 Corinthians 15, having described the wonders of the resurrection body and the reality of our continuance on the other side of the grave, Paul says, 'Therefore, my dear brothers, stand firm. Let nothing move you. Always give yourselves fully to the work of the Lord, because you know that your labour in the Lord is not in vain' (v. 58). Because he is risen, you make yourself available to work for him now. The proper response to knowing for certain that you are going to glory is to offer him your body, mind and resources here and now. The great resurrection chapter is immediately followed by chapter 16 which is all about taking up the collection. You would probably rather stay in the glory, but God wants you to deal with the offering plate. The glory will come soon enough. In this life on earth God gives you the glory on the inside, but eventually it will go from your soul to your body when it is raised in glory.

The cost

Secondly, in verses 6-19 *Paul writes of the suffering and the cost.* God paid so much to give us the glory – he gave up the Son of his heart, the best thing he had, so that we could be forgiven and share his fellowship for all eternity. Having given you everything, he is not embarrassed to ask you in principle for everything back. He says, 'Beloved daughter, beloved son, I am going to entrust you with some difficulty or pressure or pain in your life for a little while.' 1 Corinthians 10:13 tells us that God will not suffer us to be tempted, to be tested, to be tried beyond what we are able to bear, but will with the temptation provide a way of escape that we may be able to bear it. As the old saying goes, 'He tempers the wind to the shorn lamb.' But he will also say, 'You are secure for time and eternity in my love, in my providential care. Now I want you to give yourself back to me and be available to me so I can use you and sometimes let you go through the fire.'

Therefore, after restrained references to experiences in heaven, the apostle Paul talks about a thorn in the flesh that God gave him. We do not know exactly what it was, yet some commentaries seem to know more than Paul himself did. Some have suggested that maybe it was pain in his eyes, because of the reference to that in Galatians 4:15. Some scholars think that when on the Damascus road Saul of Tarsus saw the resurrection body of the Lord Jesus Christ in glory, it blinded him temporarily and may have led to permanent eye problems. But the text does not reveal specifically what the 'thorn in the flesh' was, perhaps in order that this might be a principle of general application to all Christian men and women.

When we enter into 'the fellowship of Christ's sufferings', because of our commitment to the truth, it will inevitably be costly. Maybe we suffer because of an unbelieving family member or disdainful work colleagues, or maybe because you are a Christian your children are brought under persecution. Perhaps you have financial struggles that cause problems: for example, a Christian worker was involved in a bad car accident because he was so underpaid that he could not maintain his car properly. The thorn in the flesh can take many different forms in different periods of our life.

Tracing a little glory

The apostle Paul was not a masochistic personality. He did not enjoy pain any more than any other normal person, and it certainly did not feel spiritual. Some of the most profound, fundamental, transforming works of God do not feel religious at all while they are happening. We cannot rely on our feelings to sustain us through times of trial, but instead we need to discern God's pattern of placing suffering and glory together. It is usually only with hindsight that we can begin to trace a little of the glory; we do not see it in most cases while we are going through the pressure, the hurt and the pain. It is later that we can look back on the basis of God's Word, see the pattern and say, 'Yes, it was worth it. Now I know why it seemed as if he wouldn't answer. He really was close but I thought he wasn't hearing me; I thought his face was turned away and I thought prayer wasn't working for me. But actually it was. He was just entrusting me a little longer with this pressure and suffering, because the weight of the glory would be so much more.'

It might not be until we are in heaven that we will look back over our pilgrim journey on earth, and a lot of things will begin to take shape and make sense. There will come a day, in some cases not until we reach heaven, when we can say, 'Thank you heavenly Father, for not answering the prayer when I was literally crying out for a painful situation to be taken away. You loved me and trusted me, and somehow with your grace I made it. If you'd done it the way I wanted you to in accordance with my feelings back then, there wouldn't have been this glory, these other people wouldn't have been touched and the Lord Jesus wouldn't be getting this praise today.'

A Christian student who was diabetic, had on three separate occasions said, 'Lord, surely you've got the power and I have the faith. Take away this diabetic condition, I'm going to quit using insulin.' He did not give himself the daily injection, consequently becoming seriously ill, and needing emergency insulin. Then he accepted that maybe this was like a thorn in the flesh, that it would be a permanent condition, that God had his reasons for not removing it and he would have to live with this condition. It is as if God said, 'Beloved one, it is not out of any lack of love to you, but because you have seen the glory I am going to be able to pour that much more through you. This will have to be a permanent problem in your case and I am going to have to ask you to let it stay in your flesh. I must refrain from removing it just yet.'

We all appreciate personal comfort, but there is something higher that will do both us and the world much more good than our present comfort. When we offer ourselves afresh to God, he may remove for a while some of our legitimate comforts, but so much more good will result that one day we will be in a position to thank him. Maybe heaven will shine more brightly and more pleasure will be brought to our Lord Jesus Christ.

Tenderness and compassion

We do not know exactly why Paul had this 'thorn in the flesh', although we are given a fairly clear approach to it. God refrained from removing this 'thorn in the flesh', even though Paul had asked three times for it to be taken away. Paul seems to indicate that because of the mighty mercies that God had bestowed upon him, the very high apostolic calling that he had, and the experience of seeing heaven itself, he could have succumbed to a great deal of spiritual pride. Paul accepted that it was best for him and best for the cause of the gospel that God had sent some difficulty that would remain with him all of his days, to keep him from looking at self but instead to keep him gazing on the face of Jesus Christ.

If the mighty apostle who had apparently seen God face to face was in danger of spiritual pride, are we somehow better than Paul and therefore exempt from the cost of discipleship? One of the blessings resulting from the experience of suffering is that we develop a tender, compassionate spirit for others, particularly those who may be passing through a similar trial. For example, Christian parents who have lost a child themselves are best able to bring understanding and comfort to another grieving parent going through the same distress.

'Grace is young glory'

The pattern so often seen in the Christian life of glory followed by suffering, followed by more glory, occurs again in verse 9, where God makes a wonderful promise to Paul. God says, in effect, 'My son, I am not going to take the thorn out of your flesh but I am going to do something supernatural. When any Christian is suffering for my glory in union with the Lord Jesus Christ, I am going to do something beautiful in their suffering. It is going to be more than worthwhile not only for themselves, but in some way it will bring redemptive, transforming changes in the world, little though you see it just yet. My grace will be with you and will be sufficient to hold you up; it will multiply as other people are touched with the same saving grace that ultimately will lead them to glory.' God is telling Paul that he will not be the loser by his fellowship with the cross. Instead he will gain, for when we feel we have reached the end of our human resources, grace will be there leading to glory. One of the Puritans said, 'Grace is young glory.'

In verses 9-10, Paul's triumphant conclusion is that power to transform lives comes out of this experience. God puts the glory in you, then he tests you; sometimes he keeps you in the crucible and he makes it cost you something, but the next thing you have got is power: not power for yourself, but power to bless others. Ultimately a whole culture may begin to change because of this power. Our sovereign God has all power in heaven and on earth committed into the hands of the Lord Jesus Christ, but this power is not let loose in any generation or culture until the Christians offer themselves afresh to him, saying, 'Here am I, Lord. Use me, whatever it takes. You do not have to explain. I will trust in you.' He may take them at times through dark, testing places where they feel the pain; but all the while others begin to see the glory, and the power is let loose to transform a lost and needy world. As his people accept the thorns, cultural deserts begin to blossom like the lily of the valley and rose of Sharon. For the One whom the fragrant lily and rose vaguely reflect in the wasteland, pours out his resurrection life through his people as they gaze upon him in faith.

How beautifully this stanza from an eighteenth-century Gaelic poem sums it all up. Mary MacPherson, bright Christian poetess of Badenoch, exclaimed:

'S e an Ròs e o' Shàron,
'S am Flùr e o Iesse,
'S e Gaisgeach Tréibh Iudah,
Cha chlaoidhear a neart-sa;
'S e àillteachd thar chàch
Thug mo ghràdh-sa cho mòr dha;
'S'n uair bhios e as m'fhianuis,
Bidh mi cianail ro-bhrònach.

A rather loose, free and non-literal adaptation and enlargement, a pale and broken shadow of the comely Gaelic body, follows:

Lily of the Valley, Sharon's sweet rose,
Lion of Judah, You conquer our foes.
Strong rod of Jesse, in desert you bloom;
Light in the darkness streams through your tomb.

By love you conquered; rising again,
Eden of comfort sprang from your pain.
Lord, You have raised us; break through us to shine
Triumphant glory from your face divine.

(Can be sung to the tune 'Huntingdon' in *Christian Hymns*, Evangelical Movement of Wales, 125.)

Bibliography

T S Eliot, *The Waste Land*, poem in *The Complete Poems and Plays, 1909–1950.* Harcourt Brace & Co., NY, 1980.

Herbert Schlossberg, *Idols for Destruction.* Thomas Nelson, Nashville, TN, 1983.

John Calvin, *Institutes of the Christian Religion,* ed. John T McNeill, Trans. Ford Lewis Battles. The Westminster Press, Philadelphia, 1969.

Jean Brun, *Le Retour de Dionysius.* Desclée, Paris, 1976.

E Michael Jones, *Degenerate Moderns: Modernity as Rationalized Sexual Misbehaviour*. Ignatius, San Francisco, 1993.

Paul Johnson, *The Intellectuals*. Harper & Row, NY, 1990.

Alexander Pope, 'An Essay on Man', *The Twickenham Edition of the Poems of Alexander Pope,* ed. John Butt et al., Vol. 3.1, ed. Maynard Mack, Methuen, London; Yale University Press, New Haven, 1950.

C H Spurgeon, Autobiography, Vol. 2, *The Full Harvest*. Banner of Truth Trust, Edinburgh, 1976.

John Owen, *Death of Death and the Death of Christ*. Banner of Truth Trust, London, 1963.

Jonathan Edwards, 'Resolutions', *The Works of Jonathan Edwards*, Vol. 1. Banner of Truth Trust, Edinburgh, 1974.

Jonathan Edwards, *Charity and its Fruits.* Banner of Truth Trust, London, 1969,

C S Lewis, *The Four Loves.* Harcourt Brace & Co., NY, 1960.

Professor William Milligan, *The Resurrection of Our Lord*. MacMillan, London, 1884.

Richard A Riesen, *Criticism and Faith in Late Victorian Scotland*. University Press of America, Lanham, MD, 1985.

Nicholas R Needham, *The Doctrine of Holy Scriptures in the Free Church Fathers*. Rutherford House, Edinburgh, 1991.

Dr John Zizioulas, *Being as Communion*. St Vladimir's Seminary Press, Crestwood, NY, 1993

C H Spurgeon, *Morning and Evening*. Zondervan, Grand Rapids, MI, 1965

Thomas Halyburton, *Memoirs of Thomas Halyburton*, ed. Joel R Beeke. Reformation Heritage Books, Grand Rapids, MI, 1996

E H Hamilton, poem *Afraid? Of what?* from *Poems and Sketches*. Cathay Press, Aberdeen, Hong Kong, 1963

Irving Stone, *The Agony and the Ecstasy*. Doubleday, NY, 1961

Mary MacPherson, Gaelic poem 'S e an Ros e o' Sharon', 'Togarrach Bhi Maille Ri Chriosd', *Bean Torra Dhamh: Her Poems and Life,* ed. Alexander MacRae. Alexander MacLaren and Sons, Glasgow [1935?]